She Is Empowered

A Collection of Stories of Empowering Women
from Around the World

Compiled By

Maxine Johns

Copyright © 2021 by Maxine Johns

All rights reserved. This book or any portion thereof may not be reproduced or used in any manner whatsoever without the express written permission of the publisher except for the use of brief quotations in a book review.

ISBN 978-0-646-83436-8

Edited by MHP Publishing

Layout design by Living The Empowered Life, LLC

Dedication

I would like to dedicate this book to the empowering women that have blessed my life from my earliest memories. My paternal grandmother Mabel Cohen, whose iron strength, determination and unwavering love for my father and his six siblings is legendary. My maternal grandmother Emily Jackson for her grace, strength and undying love of my mother and her five siblings, and to my mother Jenny Cohen, who encapsulates the essence of loyalty, love, passion and strength - a truly empowering woman who has not only shaped me but continues to inspire me everyday.

Thank you to the Queens in my family tree and to the Queens who have allowed me to share a snippet of their inspiring lives in this book - you are all the embodiment of empowerment!

CONTENTS

Introduction 2

Rani Bovopoulos 5

Leisyle Campbell 19

Tiana Canterbury 33

Naomi Caruana 49

Dj Dee 64

Eden Dessalegn 80

Pamela Diaz 88

Weave Dibden Neck 106

Christina Donaghue 119

Melissa Dooley 131

Mariam Freig 137

Emprezz Golding 144

Karen Griffin 151

Dora Gutierrez 161

Tracy Hinckson 168

Zaidee Jackson 175

Maya Jupiter 186

K-Sera 194

Missy Kay 199

Gladys Kibone 209

Eva Links 218

Mirrah 229

Kristelle Morin 238

Tabitha Ojeah 244

Sarah Orlarte 251

Deborah Price 263

Jannike Seiuli 272

Tamara Turrini 278

Lisa Viola 287

Phenomenal Woman by Maya Angelou

Now you understand
Just why my head's not bowed.
I don't shout or jump about
Or have to talk real loud.
When you see me passing,
It ought to make you proud.
I say,
It's in the click of my heels,
The bend of my hair,
the palm of my hand,
The need for my care.
'Cause I'm a woman
Phenomenally.
Phenomenal woman,
That's me.

Excerpt from Phenomenal Woman Poem by Maya Angelou

Introduction

I am obsessed with other peoples stories. The journey, the overcome obstacle, the triumph of adversity. There is such a beauty in success over struggle and creating a life of joy, inspiration and on your terms, that I knew this type of book was what I needed to create and these women are what the world needs to truly understand the power in their empowerment!

Sure, this isn't the first book of its kind, there have been many featuring some truly brilliant women from all walks of life, living extraordinary lives whose stories are truly inspiring. I have purchased a few in my time. However I would always feel like I couldn't totally connect with some of the women in those books as the narrative it was written in just didn't speak to me or my experiences as a woman. So I decided to dig deep and call upon the women that I am surrounded by, who inspire me, encourage me and amaze me daily with their strength and ambition and drive and passion for life. These are their stories, of triumph over adversity, of turning a simple idea into a burgeoning business success story, of turning a house into a castle , these are their stories that I believe will speak to and reach all women on so many levels.

Their stories are raw, honest, endearing and at times painful as they share truths and memories of moments long past but never forgotten. Moments of realisation, acceptance, release, forgiveness and above all else moments of self love, pride and acknowledgement of owning the women they have become and striding through life no matter what is thrown their way.

These women, like myself are from all walks of life, celebrating unique cultures and traditions from their families and bringing it all to culminate in the one major unifying similarity that bonds us all together. We have all called and for some, still call Australia home. Some have returned back to their ancestral home lands, others succumbing to wanderlust and travelling the world and for the most part a large majority of us, our feet and hearts are still firmly planted in this sunburnt country. That for the most part is such a beautiful and cultural melting pot, but it still has a ways to go in truly wearing its multicultural cape with pride. This book was created to shine a light on the varying and important narratives that so many women have and should be able to share on platforms such as this, and it is my absolute privilege to be able to create a book that houses these stories of love, acceptance and feminine power from these everyday warrior queens.

The dictionary definition of empowerment means the process of becoming stronger and more confident, especially in controlling one's life and claiming one's rights. The female definition can be defined to promote a woman's sense of self-worth, their ability to determine their own choices, and their right to influence social change for themselves and others. My hope for this book and the amazing women who shaped its narrative is just that, to continue to grow stronger and more confident in life's ever changing tapestry and for those who read it find beauty in your own truth and never be afraid to walk in your authenticity no matter what adversity or struggle you feel binds you ..... You are empowering and your story matters!

Stay shining,
Maxine xo

Rani Bovopoulos

Who is Rani? What are her origins and who would you best describe her as a woman of today?

I was born in Fiji to second generation immigrant parents. I am the younger of two children. My family background is known as Fijian Indian as my ancestors were sent from South India to work in the sugar cane farms of Fiji. They worked hard to provide for their families and created a life that was built on determination and resilience. My maternal and paternal grandparents faced challenges that a small developing country never thought they could outlive. As a result, many more successful generations have come from this and even though the Indians and the native Fijians did not always see eye to eye, the people have grown collectively to make Fiji what it is today. It is this background of my ancestors that has moulded me to never give into any adversities that come my way. In today's world, I take it upon myself to use the values of my ancestors, grandparents and parents to work hard and never give up.

What is your profession and how did you start your journey in Education?

My profession is something I sometimes feel embarrassed about answering! After school I wanted to do Law but didn't get the marks, so I went to TAFE and did Conveyancing to then make my way into University and take on further Law subjects. Through the first 6 months of the course I realised Law wasn't the pathway for me but I just kept going until I knew what I really wanted to do. An opportunity came to me to study Nursing at University. I thought this was a jackpot. My dreams of travelling while working was about to come true. I embraced nursing with so much passion and was excited about my future. My final semester approached and I was given a fabulous opportunity to go to Thailand

and live on campus at the sister university while exploring and learning about the nursing structure in their country. It was the best 2 months of my life. A memory I will never forget and so thankful that my parents allowed me to fulfill the challenge. On arrival back home a few months later, I met the man who became my husband and father of my children. Life's adventures took a halt, my dreams of working overseas as a nurse paused and my future dreams started to look different - a better different. To which I owe my fabulous friend Maxine for .....

While in my newfound relationship, I was working hard as a Registered Nurse and still wanting more out of life. So I looked into studying further and went back to uni part time while working full time and did a post graduate degree in Midwifery. This was an amazing experience and again, one I will treasure forever. I miss that part of my life very much and hope to return to it in some way in the future. Midwifery became my occupation that I adored and while working for many years and raised two children in that time. After my second child was born, the shift work and demands of midwifery began taking a toll on my life as a mother. I couldn't be the best mother to my children and felt a void. So I decided to leave and went onto working as a baby nurse at a local pharmacy. I met some incredible people, learnt so many different facets of the retail business but most importantly met some amazing mothers and gorgeous babies who looked to me for support. I truly felt like I was giving back to my local community in a small but important way, as so many women go through the toughest times in their lives when becoming a mother. This job also let me be more in tune with my children, however working retail hours became a little trying at times and I had to lean on my parents for support from time to time while my husband was focusing on his business. Two years later he approached me to come work with him so he could focus on growing his business more while I did the administration side. I never thought it would work, but somehow it did! I did this for another 2 years before we had our third child. Now my focus shifted. I have always been a working mum but now the priority was the children and how I could help more financially and be involved as much as possible for the family. So after a year off for maternity leave which was an absolute treat, I Decided to hit the books again and go back to university and do a Bachelor of Teaching in Primary school. What was I thinking?

The next year and half was intense. I studied day and night, worked through summer vacation and took on more units than I needed to, just to fast track myself and get back into the workforce. When I Graduated the elation and satisfaction was nothing like that of my 2 previous degrees. There was a different sense of accomplishment. A different sense of what this meant to me. While writing this, it brings me so much joy that I have accomplished what I have thus far and it probably comes from a little part of my heritage and what was instilled in me. Fortunately, my teaching career saw me teach many many children and many different schools. It was rewarding and challenging and I don't think I ever expected it to be. I put a lot of expectations on myself so I strived to be the best teacher and colleague. It was so humbling when teachers and schools wanted me to replace them and to take on their classes with so much trust. Unfortunately as a mature aged teacher, my opportunities didn't come easy. As a woman I felt I was always begging for work and that 'try really hard' mentality began taking a toll. I would work term upon term, weeks upon weeks and every year at the end of that year, a young graduate would take a position. It was always a sickening blow. I would feel so defeated and like a failure. I had worked so hard to get here so I didn't want to quit and let my family down. I was becoming too expensive for school budgets and last year I realised I gave so much attention to other people's children that my own children were coming second. This was not what I signed up for.

We moved to Melbourne three years ago and I have loved styling my new home. I also love cooking, but unless I made it big on Masterchef I have no chance of getting ahead in that career. After suddenly losing my dad almost two years ago, I figured that life was just too short for me to sit around and do something mundane and have life be about work. My dad spent over 10 years volunteering in our Fijian Indian community to make the new generation of Fijian Indians be proud of their heritage. He left such a huge legacy that when he passed, his mourners turned up in numbers showing me how prolific he was. I wanted to do that. I wanted to do something that allowed me self satisfaction in a small way. I wanted to be proud yet be humble just like him. So I put my head down and through some positive reinforcements, I enrolled into an Interior Design Course. Yep, I hit the books again. I still work as a casual teacher, but my focus this year is to complete my design course and do something I really enjoy. The children are getting older and independent, and the opportunities that I have with this role can be endless. I have already flipped and styled a friend's beauty store, and have 2 clients in waiting once Covid-19 passes over. It is such an exciting time. I can be my own boss for a change and who knows what I can do with this newfound career! I am scared yet excited at the same time. I'll hold my teaching registration for as long as I can, but hopefully interior design is my calling that the universe has set out for me.

You are a woman of many talents and skills which is something that is so admired and inspirational to others. At the heart of everything you do, you are always wanting to help and uplift others. You juggle being a mother to three beautiful children, supportive wife, former midwife and now a teacher always encouraging those you work amongst and with to always go the extra mile in all they do. What are your thoughts on how you have evolved in your multitude of roles and how do you balance these various nuances in your life?

Balance of work and being a mother,wife, daughter, sister....that is the mystery that surrounds women of any generation and we still haven't mastered it! I wish it was a simple answer and I wish I knew how it worked, but I must admit I am extremely lucky and fortunate that I have a supportive husband and my own personal cheer squad (kids) that push me to be the very best. This is definitely a two way relationship for us all! Put simply, the drive and passion I have for my career and daily activities come from my children. I believe that they need to see me to do something positive everyday. They never see me saying that something is difficult or that it can not be achieved. I want them to see that the world can give us some of the best opportunities that life can offer as long as you go after it.

Things can stop you in the way, but don't just settle for what you have. Sometimes things don't always work in our favour but make a positive choice out of it. I never thought I would leave midwifery, but I had to. I never thought I would leave teaching but I am exhausted and need a break. Not from teaching children, but from the bureaucracy that comes with it. I need to do something that gives me so much passion to do better and be surrounded by positivity. It was a necessity and I had to take a chance in every fork in the road because I don't want to sit back and think, I wish I did that. I want to think I did it, I tried and it did or didn't work out. It's okay to never give up and expect more from yourself. My biggest challenges have been faced in this last career change in teaching. Being a mother, older teacher, and being a female has proved the difference between me getting a full time contract to that of the opposite. But I am okay with that and I feel that every moment of my life is there for a reason. I believe that I need to grow with every experience and it just makes me a better member of society.

What do you think are the most important characteristics when it comes to creating a life on your terms and at times going against the usual stereotypes of life?

Being at peace with your decisions. I have never wanted to do something for someone else's approval, nor do I want my achievements to be what others should do. It is about you finding your own self appreciation. Most of us are working to pay bills, so that was an important facet on all my decisions. I had to make it work for our family. Every career choice has had to be for me and I had to do it on my own. Teaching has proven to be the most challenging. I had to grow a thick skin around other women who felt threatened by my positive teaching style or the fact that the students would be elated if I came to teach their class. Or when I have been rejected for job roles yet, stood tall to walk back into the school and work casually. It has been a real test to my character, but I am proud of my achievements thus far.

As a woman of creativity, passion, strength, ambition and determination, how would you best describe what success means to you and do you feel you have achieved success in your life?

Success to me comes from passion. My husband had followed his passion and it has brought him so much success and still continues to. So in many ways you could say I was envious of this for myself! Being a working mother is paramount for me, and I now want it to be more than helping with bills and more about giving me job satisfaction(although I still have to pay bills!). I have achieved success so far, but I feel I can achieve a whole lot more. I still say "when I grow up I want to be...."

What are the 5 things you cannot live without and why?

- My family - They give me a lot of drive for my daily existence.

- My kitchen - I love to cook for my family and friends. It gives me joy to see their faces when they eat and when they are satisfied while bringing us all together.

- My friends - They keep me grounded and let me talk about things to them in their individual ways so that I can be at peace in my mind.

- My yoga mat - A materialistic possession that gives me self harmony and balance

- Music - In all different genres music gives me so much satisfaction at different points of my day. Although listening to music loudly in the car is now not a thing! Really feel my age when this occurs...

The motto or mantra you live your life by?

Be true to yourself and everything around you will fall into place. Trust your gut and be your best supporter. Never adhere to anyone else's expectations of you' and believe that every achievement you make is done humbly. We can only learn from each other in this big wide uncertain world.

What advice would you give to the teenage version of yourself, 18 years old and just about to embark on your life's journey?

Travel. Defy the odds and set sail a little. Push yourself and good things will fall into place. Trust that going against the grain is okay. Growing up in an ethnic family whose parents immigrated with fears and aspirations for their children, I never wanted to disappoint them. So my dreams of not conforming to a nine to five job or a career with stability was just that, a dream. I also believe that failure can come from 'not trying' so it's important to fail to be able to learn and arise from the different opportunities. I wish I was a risk taker when I was younger.

Three songs that speak to your soul?

I'm going to have fun with this question!

1. Sisqo - Thong song- because it was the first song my husband and I danced to when we first met (hahaha awkward!)

2. Jodeci - All My Life - because I thought I was so cool that I loved Jodeci until I met my husband

and there was a whole other RnB genre I never knew existed (omg so lame).

3. Kelis - Milkshake - because I would listen to this song very very loud in my little car and thought I was the baddest girl in Blacktown (haha haha so delusional). There is a theme here - I thought I was so cool! Omg.....

What are you most proud of yourself for and why?

Creating my family. I am proud that my children see their mother as a go-getter, and their father as a high achiever yet stay as humble and true to ourselves as best as we possibly can. I want my daughter to believe that anything is possible and my boys to know that they do not have to be a sole provider nor settle for things to be 'okay'. It's important that they see their parents as high achievers so they can tackle life with positivity and know that it takes their own hard work to get there. We believe that our parenting may not be everyone's cup of tea, but we want our children to be good humans in society and to treat each other with respect. I tell them many times they only have each other in this world because their bond will never surpass anyone else's. I have noticed over time, that our family fits in a very different mould to that of both sides of the families and I couldn't be prouder of my children. Life will throw many obstacles and they need to learn that they can only achieve what they want in life with the guidance that we provide for them.

Leisyle Campbell

Who is Leisyle Campbell? What are her origins and who would you best describe her as a woman of today?

Who is Leisyle Campbell? Well I was born to South African parents who immigrated to Australia to flee from the Apartied. I am the oldest of two siblings. I have hard working parents who have always taught me great morals and also how to be respectful, I am very grateful for how my parents raised me with the right amount of rules and boundaries and also keeping our culture in mind which I always appreciated. My parents growing up took my brother and I back to South Africa for the first time when I was 9 years old, I remember this trip so distinctively as it was a real eye opener to how sheltered and serene growing up in Australia can be. Our first stop was to relatives in Johannesburg, South Africa and my Aunty and Uncle to whom which we were staying with for the duration of our stay in Johannesburg had a property which was within a close distance to the township Soweto. I would never forget that during this time it was the tail end of the apartheid and probably the main reason that my parents waited this long to take up back to their country of origin, and being so close to Soweto it was scary for us at the time because it was just a ball of fire and also full of sounds of war and conflict, which was ultimately the signs that the country was still coming to rest. It was also in this first trip that I realized how grateful I was that my parents had decided to raise us in Sydney, Australia.

This realization became real when we were on a daily outing in South Africa and I saw these tiny little African boys in a town center sitting on the side of the road sniffing a tin can. I turned to my uncle and asked "What are they doing Uncle Patrick "and he explained to me that they are sniffing the glue to stop them from feeling hungry. I knew in that moment that a lot of the values that my parents had already started teaching me had come evidently from their upbringing and environment in South Africa. Lessons like " There are a lot of people worse off in the world than you" " There are starving kids in Africa, you better eat the food given to you" these were all playing through my head as I looked at the little African boys and knew that I need to be grateful every day for what I have. I think a lot of these lessons from my parents, my experiences in South Africa and also my life experiences have molded me to the woman I am today. Being GRATEFUL is something that I do every day and also teaching my kids now to do as well. Also giving back and paying it forward is something very much ingrained in me, my mum especially is always ready to help anybody and give back and I also very much am always looking for ways to help or give back. The woman I am today though is definitely something I am proud of if I was to describe myself in a few words I would say I am courageous, nurturing, creative.

What is your profession and how did you start your creative journey?

My profession, at its core, is that of a Graphic Designer specializing in print press design, but I have evolved into a Graphic Designer with my love of Wedding Stationery. I I own and operate Love Campbell Wedding Stationery & Design. I started my creative journey when I left school. The first course that I completed after my Higher School Certificate was a Cert 4 in Drawing Fundamentals. I had always been interested in all of the creative subjects in school and spent all of my lunch breaks in high school in the art classroom instead of being outside in the playground at lunch. It is then the pressure I had from what I would consider to be my "old school" parents who started to put on the pressure after I left my first TAFE course to make sure that I was studying something that was going to give me a "good job" which is I guess thinking of it now all I could expect from my hard working parents which did find it hard to understand their creative daughter. It was from the pressure from my parents and also my need to be in the creative field that I stumbled upon the field of Graphic Design. After getting approval from my parents that this was a "good job" field to pursue I enrolled into an Associate Diploma in Graphic Design at Liverpool TAFE.

I was completing my Associate Diploma in Graphic Design and really enjoying it until I became ill in my second year of TAFE to which I had a whole semester off. When I was all better and ready to come back to TAFE I had really missed too much of my classes and had to defer my second year of TAFE. Feeling unmotivated and also not knowing what I wanted to do with myself I decided to go and work full time and have a break from studying. I spent the next 4 years working full time at Sanity Music, then one day I got invited to one of my old TAFE colleagues' weddings. I turned up to the wedding to enjoy the celebration and there at the wedding were 3 of my old TAFE teachers ready with enrolment papers to enrol me back into TAFE. They were ready to pin me down and demand I come back and complete my Diploma at TAFE, and so I re-enrolled at the wedding and went back to TAFE. My Graphic Design Diploma really opened up my eyes on a different way to be creative and it is what really started my journey to where I am today.

You are a woman of many talents and skills which is something that is so admired and inspirational to others. You are also a mother of two beautiful children and an entrepreneur of an amazing home based event stationery business that is highly regarded in the Australian Bridal industry. What are your thoughts on your motherhood journey and how have you made the balance of home based-career and parenting mesh?

Looking back on it now I am so thankful that I did start my business full time when my first son Keenan was born. The reason being is that when you become a mumma you realize the amount of strength and courage we have as women. I started my business full time in 2012 when my first baby came into the world, I had stumbled into Wedding and Event Stationery as a hobby leading up to me starting my business by friends and friends of friends asking me to do their wedding invitations as they knew that I was a Graphic Designer. By the time I had completed my 5th set of wedding invitations for a client I knew that is what I wanted to do with my career and also the niche I wanted to concentrate on with my design. I always said to myself leading up to becoming a mum that I would like to work from home and run my own Wedding Stationery Business. When my first son entered this world of course I was full time mum and learning how to be a mum but by the time my son was 5 months old I was already thinking about my next move and also how I was going to bring in a source of income and also stay home with my son being so little and still needing very much his mum.

This of course was my biggest hiccup when it came to taking the leap of faith for my business to go from hobby to business. How was I going to do this without putting any strain on the household we needed to keep stable for our new biggest responsibility, my son. And so this is how I ended up entering the Government funded program called NEIS which stands for New Enterprise Incentive Scheme. This is a Government supported program which essentially puts you through Cert 4 n Small Business Management in 6 weeks where the course normally takes 1 year and then furthermore you get a small business mentor for 1 year and also receive a support payment from NEIS to support you through your first year of business. I did all of this to launch my business from hobby to business and did this with a 5 month old in two.

Fast forward to today I have an established business that is going 8 years strong now. It hasn't been the easiest journey as I did all this while becoming a mum twice. Balancing parenthood and a work from home business was a constant see saw of commitment between my own dreams and also caring for the most precious things in the world for me. I took on the model that I would grow my business as my babies grew so the way that I essentially made it work in the baby years of my childrens lives was to take on the amount of work that could work around the commitment of my kids. This worked perfectly and was seeing my business take on a good surge until I found out that my daughter Alika at 15 months old was being diagnosed with Early Autism. This of course was an interesting time in both my journey in motherhood and also in business. After taking a good 6 months to digest what my new normal was going to look like with my daughter moving ahead I continued my dream of being a mumpreneur but still continuing the delicate see saw of business and babies.

My daughter's diagnosis of course led the see saw to lean more towards the babies side of my life but this world of ASD was new to me and I was navigating it the best way I knew how to educate myself and stay positive.

I learnt a valuable lesson though in 2016/2017 when I started to have consistent recurring anxiety attacks, now I had had anxiety in my 20s but this anxiety was a whole new ball game and was attacking my body in different ways that I knew before. It was crippling, I was fearful of everything and most of all my see saw of babies and business was in a frantic motion of up and down on both sides as I tried to keep my head above water and continue to navigate babies and business and now ANXIETY. It was then when I ended up in hospital with chest pains that I realised that the biggest element that was missing from my see saw was me. I was the steady structure in the middle of the see saw and that was crumbling and not working anymore so my two main commitments of my business and my babies were not going to work if the structure and centre of the see saw was not working. So there I was in the hospital dealing with yet another body reaction to the beast that is anxiety and I made myself a promise when I was in that hospital bed that I wasn't going to end up here again. I left the hospital that night and faced my fears, faced that this anxiety was not going to kill me, I had two full nights of no sleep and my own chest squeezing itself so hard it felt like my chest was in a vice. But I stayed there and told myself I was going to beat this, I was going to let this defeat me. Through this time I had to learn how to rebalance the see saw, and the first way I had to do that was to take some time out to heal myself. In all of my constant balancing I lost the most important part of the see saw which was me so I took time out from my business which was the hardest decision I have ever had to make and learn how to rebalance and centre myself and also of course look after my babies.

The most important lesson I have learned through parenting/motherhood and also being an entrepreneur is self care, making sure I am looking after myself spiritually, mentally, physically and social/ emotionally. If I take care of me then all of my success will be free to soar

What do you think are the most important characteristics when it comes to creating a life on your terms and at times going against the usual stereotypes of life?

One of the most important characteristics I have learnt is to be brave and to face your fears, our self talk can be filled with a lot of negativity and also fears to stop us from reaching our highest potential. One thing that I always try to do is to do something that makes me uncomfortable and I have found that every fear or being uncomfortable that I have faced has led me even more to creating the life that I have always wanted. Another characteristic is self belief , this is a big one. You need to have self belief as the power in the engine to keep moving you forward especially when you are going against every grain that has been known of you before. The journey of motherhood alone is a lonely and brave journey but add being an entrepreneur and doing your life's passion you need to have that self love, self belief and most of all celebrate how UNIQUE you are.

As a woman of creativity, strength, ambition and genuinity, how would you best describe what success means to you and do you feel you have achieved success in your life?

What success means to me is to see something that is an idea in my head come to life and then flourish and grow and most of all be successful. This is how my business started. It was an idea and I made the steps and kept persisting until the idea grew and came to life. Today in 2020 I believe that I am very successful and also grateful for how successful I have been. All of my creative ideas are unique and executed with attention to detail and finished with impeccable flaws to them. That is what I pride myself with especially in the wedding industry where I am creating for a couple the most important day of their life and that I get that honor of helping their dream day come to life. Being creative is often a misunderstood personality trait and we can often be looked upon as being a bit airy fairy or because a lot of mainstream society don't understand the lengths we go to as creatives to execute, plan and create our ideas we are often misused and under valued by the normal society. But I believe that I have owned my creative trait really well and celebrate the uniqueness of it which in hand has turned into my own success.

What are the 5 things you cannot live without and why?

1. My kids : my kids are my strength which keep me going. If I have a deadline and I feel like I can't possibly physically complete the deadline, I always look at my kids and know that as well as myself I do this for them and also for the ability to be at home with them and see all the special moments I would miss if I was at work.

2. Family : Whether it be my parents which I have always tried to get them to understand my creativity and they may not understand it but they are still the most supportive parents and also my husband which is a fellow creative and also his support and also having a fellow creative to bounce off is priceless

3. Yoga : yoga is my saviour when it comes to keeping me centred, disciplined and calm. I start my day with Yoga every morning to have that moment to myself and refresh and start the day with a zen energy.

4. Friends : social and emotional wellbeing I realised becoming a mum how important that is and also being a mum of a child with Autism Spectrum Disorder. My friends are a must to have a debrief or vent , but most of all let me know that I am not alone in this world of being a mum and also a mumpreneur.

5. 70% Dark Chocolate : it is my one guilty pleasure each day, which is not even really that guilty because it is really good for you. But I need to have my 70% Dark Chocolate.

The motto or mantra you live your life by?

My mission or motto is to live with inner peace, joy and happiness through effective self management, ease and discipline. And we also have a family mantra which is simple to "be proactive"

What advice would you give to the teenage version of yourself, 18 years old and just about to embark on your life's journey?

My main advice to my 18 year old self is to not live life in the shadows and to celebrate who you are and also celebrate how unique you are.

What are you most proud of yourself for and why?

I am most proud of myself for having self belief and also facing any of my fears which in hand has led to a successful wedding business now of 8 years and has also allowed me to branch my business out into three branches which is Seasonal Stationery and also Logo and Corporate Design.

Tiana Canterbury

Who is Tiana Canterbury? What are her origins and who would you best describe her as a woman of today?

Tiana Canterbury is a woman who is forever evolving. I am a passionate, driven, creative and artistic being that loves to learn, teach and share my craft with others. I was born 4th of September 1980 in Cape Town, South Africa. Both my parents Aubrey and Althea Canterbury are still to this day, hard-working, dedicated parents who love their three children and now six grandchildren and their sports. Since I can remember, my parents, my brother and I would be on the softball field every weekend and weekdays at practice. Both parents represented SACOS Team (South African Coloured team) during the Apartheid. My father and his brother were the pioneers of baseball and softball in the coloured community. My mother was the captain of the SSA and represented South Africa in the World Masters, and my eldest brother Jude (7years older) represented SACOS in baseball at 16 years old. Later on when we moved to Australia, my middle brother Chad (2 years older) represented NSW in both softball and baseball.

When I look back, the dedication and love my family had towards softball, baseball, and their community was the start of the fire within me. I learnt the importance of self-discipline, training / practise, mindset, passion, and to always give 100%. That passion for me was evident through dance. From many stories from my parents, brothers, family and friends who I don't remember, would tell me that at the age 18 months old, I would copy every dance move on TV and obsessed with Janet Jackson. At the age of 7, I would entertain the crowd at events with my dance combos, get the kids in the neighbourhood and create routines and have them in positions, ready for our mini shows to entertain the kids in the street. I was so in my zone with dance that the neighbourhood gangs would ask my parents if I could perform with their dance crews at events or parties. It makes me laugh remembering how far I've come to dance.

However it wasn't all smooth sailing living in South Africa. When I was four years old, our former maid and her friends abducted me from my home, and I was found days later by a nun in the backyard of an unknown person in a township called Langa. That experience was one of the scariest moments for my parents and also the main reasons to immigrate to Australia. I've cracked my skull from sliding headfirst down the stairs and even been told that I had childrens arthritis and that later on in life, I might not be physically able to be active or play sports. This prediction was clearly far from the truth. In 1989 at the age of 9, we migrated to Australia. The main two things that took a minute to adjust to was, one, seeing so many white people everywhere with weird accents and, two, how lenient the teachers were and no one got the cane, ruler or belt. My brother and I were cheering and at the same time, shocked. Back in South Africa, you would get the cane or ruler, if you didn't clean under your nails and your ears, if you spoke back to a teacher, didn't do your homework etc. and the one thing I used to get the cane for was, not being able to read Afrikaans. This was the one subject I would start sweating walking into the class. It didn't take long for me to adjust to Australian life or make friends. With my love of dance and sharing dance, I made friends quickly with kids in the schools and other surrounding schools. School really wasn't my thing. My parents would be at the office every other week due to me missing days because I was either away doing shows or just skipping it to be amongst the other dancers or creatives, whom mind you, were way older than me.

After finishing high school, I started working straight away with my mother at Westpac Bank and doing dance gigs on the side. It wasn't until I began to make my own money, enjoy being a young adult, going out without the pressures from my parents, performing and booking serious dance gigs when at 19 years old I found out I was pregnant with my first child Lexus. The news came as a major shock to everyone. I immediately stopped dancing, got married, moved out of home and 1.5 years later filed for divorce. 2003 was a significant turning point for me as I took a chance on myself and decided to focus on dance and choreography full time as a single mother. I also met my love, Mike Champion. In 2007 we had a son Rome and then 2013 our daughter Myka. From day one till now has been one extraordinary journey of incredible experiences, many uh ha moments and lessons and major highs and lows. When I look back, there are many things I wouldn't want for my life but nothing I would change, and through all the adversity and struggles, I truly discovered my inner strength. The woman I am today strives to live in truth, no time constraints and just love.

What is your profession and how did you start your journey in the entertainment industry?

I am a Choreographer, Movement Director, Scene Expert for Red Bull dance, Manager / Agent for mychildren, and I have my program mentoring dancers, singers and actors transitioning into the entertainment industry. After many years of dancing for the neighbourhood kids in SA and high school events, my brother Chad, 15, friend Anita, 16 and myself, 13 at the time, created a group named TAC. We started by performing as support act shows at Wonderland Amusement Park before the international and Aussie acts would come out and perform for the crowd. From this gig, we met many amazing people in the industry who put us on shows with Montell Jordan, Kaylan, a Lighter Shade of Brown and many memorable artists at such a young age.

I did weekly gigs during my high school years with the Kaylan brothers, Darren and Dennis from 13 - 18 years old. I grew up extremely fast, but extremely necessary as this was the period I learnt so much about colourful characters in the industry. I must say, this is where my "DONT TAKE NO SHIT" attitude came about. I had a break from dance between 19 to 21 to take care of my daughter Lexus. Once I made that move to dance full-time after my divorce, it was a bumpy start at first but then found my groove booking gigs again and getting my dance skills up. I did podium dancing at one of Sydney's finest night spots, CAVE Nightclub. Doing podium dancing was where I met incredible DJ's, built my knowledge of music, learnt how to read the crowd and perfected the art of performing in front of a live audience that stood all up in my business. Hahaha I also taught at the well known Hip Hop dance studio in Australia, Urban Dance Centre, director Juliette Verne. It such a short period of returning to dance, I performed with artists such as Nitty, Chingy, Ja rule, Guy Sebastian for the ARIA and many more. I then got a phone call from

Channel 10 producers of SYTYCD to choreograph a dancehall routine, and the video had the highest views and controversy for TV at the time. From then on, I choreographed all four seasons. In between performing for artist and teaching, I also choreographed all of Mike's shows. Working with Mike was a time where I could explore my creativity as a creative director and put together all his visual and stage concepts.

After my second child Rome, I did many movies such as Great Gatsby, The Matrix and The Mask. I then created my own all-female African Dance group SAEA BANYANA. My vision for this group was to showcase our power as women through our cultures, movement and style. We went viral on youtube with my choreography to Elephant Man's track Swagga. The journey with the ladies was an exciting one, especially having young African girls look up to us and follow our journey. The African Australian community gave us all their support, and that was a proud moment for me starting my dance journey in South Africa as a little girl. We then auditioned for a dance TV Show called Everybody Dance Now and made it through as one of Kelly Rowland's teams and won the section. Being able to share our culture on TV was another special moment for me to choreograph and share gumboot dance on an Australian network.

In 2011, I worked with Janet Jackson on a three-day shoot with Jake Nava (director of Beyonce & Kanye West video clips). The commercial shoot was for Nutrisystem that Janet was representing. It was only Janet, Jake Nava and myself on set for three days straight. I got to learn so much from Jake Nava on directing and insight on what a perfectionist and kind hearted human Janet Jackson is.

An experience I will never forget as this was a dream of mine from a very young age to work with her. And I did. In 2013 I had my third child Myka. From then I choreographed the Closing Ceremony for Dalai Lama, Macklemore's NRL half time performance, choreographer on Dance Boss, for Timomatic, Jess Mauboy, Stan Walker and many more. I then opened up my own dance studio, Your Hip Hop Class, in the Sydney and Campbelltown area with hundreds of students that came through. I toured Australia and NZ with the MADIBA musical, created my agency for TV and Commercials that represents my family and other talents in Sydney. And now I am the Scene Expert for Red Bull where I scout Aussie talents to compete in one the worlds biggest dance competitions. There are so many incredible jobs, shows and experiences I haven't added in the above but not forgotten.

You are a woman of many talents and skills which is something that is so admired and inspirational to others. You are also a mother of three incredible children that are not only amazing extensions of yourself but are becoming stellar examples of children with drive, dream and above all soul. When you look at your kids what are your thoughts on your motherhood journey and how have you made the balance of career and parenting mesh?

Motherhood has indeed been one incredible journey. I know and feel that God and the universe have gifted me with my children in order for me to become the woman and human being I am meant to be on this earth. My children individually came into my life at times when there were lessons to be learnt in my own life. They have helped strengthen my relationship with myself as a mother and teacher. Being a young mum at the age of 19 years old, I didn't know who I was; I didn't know what self-love meant or to love someone else entirely. After divorcing Lexus's father, pursuing my dreams, being a single mum and always on the go, there was a disconnection in our relationship up until her teenage years. Before Lexus hit her adolescent years, in my mind, I thought our relationship was perfect. My child was respectful; everyone told me I raised a well-mannered child, we looked the part, dressed well and always up for a laugh. But behind closed doors, I had a strict approach with Lex because I felt at the time that I didn't want her to make bad decisions in life and allow others to think that she was weak. It wasn't until Lexus was in year 8 or 9 when she stood up to me in an argument and shared all her honesty and told me how she felt about our relationship, she told me what she wanted from me and that it was just pure and simply love. This moment hit me so hard in many ways. It made me look deeper within and to why I am here on earth. In such a short time, our relationship grew stronger, and on levels, I just can't explain.

Lexus is 20 years old but is the most inspiring woman to me. She lives and speaks with strength, passion, empathy and love. Lex has the fighter side of me but knows how to be present and show love to everyone around her. We still to this day say that she is the mother in the family because she taught me how to love, show love and receive love. My son Rome, who is 14 years old now, has taught me that communication and being understood is key to building a strong relationship in families. He is the only person in the family, other than Mike Champion, that doesn't say too much, but when he does, I will stop whatever I am doing to listen and whole heartily hear, feel and see him. Our relationship has shaped the way I approach teaching young students and understanding them before offloading what I know. Miss Myka, the baby of the family, has taught me that time does not matter and to stop and be present. This lesson has been a big one for me since she has come into our lives and helped me balance my career and being a mother. As I'm getting older and truly knowing who I am, I know that my kids and Mike are my number one priority, they are what makes me happy inside, they are the support and reason I love and do what I do. Knowing this puts everything into perspective and makes it easy to balance my career and family life.

I am now very confident and comfortable with putting mine, and my family needs first, stopping to be present with the kids and Mike and not allowing time, my outside environment, others and work to set me off balance.

What do you think are the most important characteristics when it comes to creating a life on your terms and at times going against the usual stereotypes of life?

The characteristics I thought were important to me say ten years ago would have been; to work twice as hard, take all opportunities that present itself, be the noise in the industry, do and be whomever you have to be to achieve your goals and to have that "Show them what you all about" attitude. Did this work for me back then? Hell yeah, it did, but my happiness for what I achieved was always short-lived and at the time would feel like there was no purpose. Don't get me wrong; I am incredibly grateful for every opportunity and all my achievements through my life, career and family. Still, I never felt like those characteristics and actions wholeheartedly fulfilled me and were on my terms. When I look back, it was all ego-driven and living up to others expectations and perception of my family and me. Today I will say I strongly commit to balancing my energy internally and allowing it to freely create my external world and the experience living it, without ego or the emotions from the past.

As a woman of passion, strength, ambition and loyalty, how would you best describe what success means to you and do you feel you have achieved success in your life?

Success to me is overcoming myself and self expectation as well as the expectation of others. It is important to me to set a clear intention and allow my intention to create freely in order for me to feel successful. To me success is an ongoing journey of internal growth and commitment. It is a commitment that must be governed by self love and unconditional love for others and life. As long as I'm taking the time to focus on these things, I feel successful.

What are the five things you cannot live without, and why?

1. My children and Mike - They keep me grounded; they are my lessons, my joy and happiness. When I went on tour with the Madiba Theatre show for five months, this was the time I realised that I could not function properly without my family by my side.

2. Daily Meditation - This is my time to settle the mind and body into coherent energy, centre

myself and elevate my emotions before taking on the day.

3. Exercising - I love the push and feeling the burn physically when exercising. It makes me feel alive.

4. Growth - I love listening and reading self-help books/podcasts and having deep conversations that will spark ideas, opinions and evolve the mind.

5. CHOCOLATE - Chocolate is something I cannot give up, no matter how hard I tried to. I have to have chocolate at least once in the day. Haha, I love the texture and obviously the taste. Who doesn't like chocolate, though? And if you don't, you need to meditate that right now into your life. Haha, you are missing out.

The motto or mantra you live your life by?

"Life responds not to what we want; It responds to who we are being".

I think about this when I wake up, before I go to bed, before entering a room or meeting and when interacting or communicating with my family and others, and I ask myself "What am I broadcasting (consciously or unconsciously) daily?"

What advice would you give to the teenage version of yourself, 18 years old and just about to embark on your life's journey?

- Love, learn and be present with yourself and your child first and foremost

- You are loved - Be kinder to yourself

- Don't let fear stop you doing what matters most

- Treat life like a practice. We won't always get it right or perfect. Just be entirely yourself

- You are not alone - What you are doing now will contribute to who you will become - The world is bigger than you think.

- Trust your artist's brain.

- Chase knowledge, not acceptance

- Don't worry about tomorrow. - You can wait -

- Patience and timing - You are capable of so much more than you think.

- Learn money management skills

- Travel, Travel & TRAVEL

Three songs that speak to your soul?

- Nothing Even Matters By Lauren Hill feat D'Angelo - This song reminds me to just be present in love.

- Sweet Life By Mike Champion - The lyrics to this song is spot on and gets me every time. When I'm feeling confused or low, this is my go-to song, to remind me it is all ok and to not be so hard on myself.

- Find Love By Mike Champion - Ok it might seem like this is a trend and I'm just choosing Mike Champion songs, haha but in all honesty, this song reminds that you are not alone and to reach out to others and share the love.

What are you most proud of yourself for and why?

I'm most proud of the daily growth in my relationship with my children and Mike, where we can speak openly about our fears, insecurities, strengths etc. and unapologetically be who we want in the presence of each other. I'm also proud of the parents both Mike and myself have become and the relationship we share without losing our individual identities, dreams and goals.

Naomi Caruana

Who is Naomi? What are her origins and who would you best describe her as a woman of today?

I am very open and I love to engage with people, find out who they are. I learnt a long time ago, that most people like to talk about themselves so I find it easy to ask people open questions that aren't too personal and depending on the response, can usually connect with that person on some level. I think I am very empathic, I can try and relate other people's situations to mine so as to better understand them and myself. I was born in

Sydney's southern suburbs to parents Leslie and Elaine Elliott who lived in Cronulla with my older brother, Nathan, three at the time. My baby sister, Sarah, came along 22 months after me. My dad was a fitter and machinist and my mum was a district manager for Avon Beauty Products and she was very successful at this. My sister, brother and I all did classical ballet as well as tap and jazz and it seemed that we spent a lot of our childhood doing this. We would dance 3 days during the week and all day on Saturday. We all stopped in our teens and I discovered then that I loved to sing. My Dad joined our church choir (he has a beautiful baritone) and I joined him. I loved singing and would eventually have my voice trained, not for a profession, but just for fun. When I was living at home with my parents, my Mum could tell if there was something wrong with me because she said I would stop singing around the house. She always knew I was happy if I was singing..... I still sing to day but only at home with my boys which they don't seem to mind and I encourage them to sing, dance or play an instrument -anything to tap into their creative sides, I think this builds confidence in children and can help get through the teen years, when insecurities creep in. I didn't move out of home until I was 26, which I feel was very late, and when I did, I moved into a shared house in Redfern with a whole lot of backpackers. This was a very happy time and I call this "My Bohemian" period. A lot of night outs, parties, festivals and meeting interesting characters. This period was also the start of my real confidence and independence and an awakening to what type of life I wanted for myself. Previously I had been very insecure, even though I made friends easily, I always felt a little paranoid and judged and I had severe body issues and low self-esteem. I often found men that would hone in on these insecurities and manipulate me and our lives together to enhance drama and thrive on their own narcissistic tendencies……then I met Jason. I was 32 and he was just 23, eight years my junior. On first meeting him and then getting to know him within a few short weeks, I realised that age didn't matter and there is someone out there for everyone, you just have to be patient. Jason was and still is a very mature soul, he is level headed and honest and open and very loving. To me at the time, he seemed to have his shit together and he still does. He is motivated in everything he does, and this motivates me in everything as well. I am what you would call a nester. I love house work, cooking, sewing and nurturing and Jas compliments me in this in that he has pride in his home and is constantly trying to improve it. He is the same with our boys, always encouraging them, very patient with their questions and conversation. A very loving man, in a quite masculine way that I find very sexy.

What is your profession? How did you end up in the industry you work in and what do you love about what you do?

I work Strata Management but originally, I just wanted to be a secretary and had the opportunity to get my certificate through a traineeship through TAFE. I was hired as a temp at BCS Strata Management in 2002 in Sydney CBD. After 3 months, I was hired on a permanent basis as their receptionist and would later go on to be the Personal Assistant to the Director, then the CFO and eventually to the CEO. In 2009 I had my first son and after maternity leave, in 2010, I was very fortunate enough to get a part time position in our BCS Miranda Branch. This enabled me to be with my baby and then after about a year in 2011, Jas and I welcomed our second son and again after maternity leave, I went back to our Miranda branch part time until my youngest went to school, where I have been full time since. What

I love about what I do is helping people living in communal living. It has its challenges but it also has its rewards. Such as knowing that people's investments are being managed to a high standard.

You are a woman of many talents and skills which is something that is so admired and inspirational to others. You are a devoted wife and mother of 2 beautiful boys and your outlook on life has always been so positive and encouraging. You have gone through some very challenging times, surviving a terrible breast cancer ordeal that has seen you come out the other side as a warrior queen with your incredible attitude towards your surgery and treatment. How was that experience for you and how do you view your role as a mother and woman having survived something as huge as that?

We were driving through our suburb to go to soccer with the boys one morning in 2018, and the car in front of us had a sticker on the window "Real Chicks Check Tits" and I remember thinking "Oh, Tits, that a rude word" and then hahahaha "Tits" and then "That rhymes" and that night I did just that, I checked my tits. Ironically, I did find a lump in my right breast in 2019, around Jasons birthday in June. I remember feeling it for a few weeks and then saying to Jas, 'feel that, what do you think" and he said "get that shit sorted" and I was thinking....man now I gotta get a Drs referral, take time off work, have a mammogram, which is not fun! As it was, my Dr saved my life as she also requested a biopsy of the lump while I was having the scans. The scans did not show anything abnormal in my breast, but you could feel the lump and when the Dr did the biopsy I remember saying to her when she put the needle into the lump to draw out cells out "I can't feel that needle going in, it feels like your sticking something into a cork" She asked me if I had children when she was cleaning up after the biopsy and when I said I had 2 little boys she wiped her hands and as she walked out she said "well, all the best" and I thought, that's a funny thing to say. That was on the Wednesday and on Friday morning my Drs office called and asked if I could go in that morning before 12.00pm and I put them on hold while I asked my boss if I could leave early, then the receptions said " can you also bring your husband" and that's when I knew it was cancer.

The process of having the lump removed was not daunting at all as the nurses at the hospital were amazing, explaining everything that was happening every step of the way. I am a very positive person and optimistic, so at this time I was thinking " I'll get the lump removed and that will be it". It wasn't until we went the following Tuesday to see my Breast Surgeon to get the results, in my mind, all clear, that the Dr said they found pre-cancerous cells on every margin of my breast. I didn't know what that meant at first, but as the Dr kept talking about going and removing as much of the breast he could around the margins to get all the cells and that he may not get them all and may have to go back to carry out a mastectomy, that I realised,I had to have a mastectomy. I kept it together in the Drs office, but when Jas and I got out into the hall to go to the car , I looked at him and said "I'm going to lose my breast" and it hit me. Straight away, he was amazing and said "oh baby girl, you're not losing your breast, you're saving your life" and that was a game changer. He was right, everything from that point on was not about me but about saving my life for my family. The good thing about my Cancer is that it didn't spread into my lymph nodes, which I am so very grateful for which meant the cancer did not spread through my body and was contained in the lump.

My recovery has been positive and Jason was the greatest driver for this. It was hard after the surgery as my strength was taken and he had to help me with everything from showering to dressing and I was so high on pain treatment that I couldn't work. But with his positive attitude and daily reassurance, I was getting better and stronger, and it wasn't long before I was up and about again doing things for myself. The first two weeks after the operation would have been the hardest as I had drains in my wounds. My youngest was very happy the day the drains were removed and he said "does this mean I can sit and cuddle you now?" Once I was well and strong again, I was lucky enough to be able to work from home and then I went back to work while doing my radiation treatment,which was 5 days of treatment for 5 weeks. I was grateful this didn't affect my mood and I wasn't sick from the radiation, but by the end of the treatment my arm and breast were severely burnt, and I had to have dressings every day until the burns healed. The last of the burns repaired on New Years Eve for 2020 and I could go swimming with my boys over the holidays. My boys were so amazing through all of this. Jas and our family and friends did so much to help the boys not feel as if my convalescence was frightening and that it didn't impact them too much. They were very gentle around me and very loving, happy just to cuddle me, they still are.

Even though I have finished my treatment for cancer, I am still only in the middle of my journey, because my Cancer is hormonal based, I am in the process of having my ovaries shut down chemically and then removed altogether to stop my body producing estrogen and protogine, which is believed to have caused the Cancer. Putting my body into early Menopause is a whole new challenge in itself, the hot flushes, mood swings, tiredness, the list goes on. I have a really great doctor who is giving me the right treatment to help with all of this. I am also on medication for the next 5 -10 years called Tomaxafin, which is a cancer receptor medication to help prevent the cancer from returning. This, I am hoping, will do the trick for good. I am also waiting to have breast reconstruction on my right breast to get some natural symmetry back into my body. I am opting for a Trans flap reconstruction, which involves removing fat from my abdomen and moving this up into my right breast area along with various veins and arteries to keep that fat healthy. I then have a tummy tuck and I get a new belly button. This operation is HUGE, more than the mastectomy and I am a little frightened going into it as I am fully healed from the mastectomy and don't really want to go backwards in my health/strength. But I have to keep reminding myself that I am a fast healer and it won't be long before I am walking the dog with my boys and Jason again and riding out bikes as a family. This harder surgery is more beneficial in the long run as it is using my own body to heal as opposed to prosthetics. Having my breast removed has made me appreciate my body more than ever. Going from having such terrible body distortion as a young woman, to loving my body expanding while growing two beautiful life forms and now to seeing how amazing my body really is by surviving this Cancer and how quickly I can heal. It has made me see that I am beautiful and strong and need to keep me healthy- mentally, physically and spiritually.

What do you think are the most important characteristics when it comes to creating a life on your terms and at times going against the usual stereotypes of life?

A plan is important in creating what you want – a goal. I do believe in listening to both the positive and the negative as the negative can make you stronger. As a blonde and having an upbeat personality, I have always been thought of as a "Bubble Head". This has made me try harder to prove to myself that I am intelligent and that my voice does matter. Jason is my greatest supporter in making me believe that I am not a bubble head – this description of me really upsets him as he knows that I am a great planner and executor of ideas and goals. If you have a want or a need that you think will make you happy and it doesn't hurt anyone, give it a go. Don't listen to the naysayers or rather do and show them that they are wrong.

As a woman of passion, strength, loyalty and compassion, how would you best describe what success means to you and do you feel you have achieved success in your life?

I think success in life comes from confidence in yourself. My confidence as a young woman was shot and it wasn't until after leaving a mentally abusive relationship that I realised that I needed to look at me and relax and enjoy/love myself as a person. And that still stands today – if someone makes me feel less than confident, I take stock in things that are important to me – my unconditional love for my family and their love for me. The home that Jas and I have built together with our family and friends, who are genuine and love us without judgement. I tell my boys how lucky I am to have them as I was considered old (by my mother anyway) to have children.

My success is having a family and having a man who cherishes me – I never thought I would be calm or confident in myself to have those things. Self loathing and or insecurity are ugly traits and only those that thrive on that ugliness seek that out. Overcoming those two roadblocks have made me a more complete woman. This is not everyone's measure of success and I don't judge anyone who does not want that type of life. This is my success, not theirs.

What are the 5 things you cannot live without and why?

- My family – they fill my void and give me purpose.
- My mascara – I have very faint eyelashes and need to paint them before I leave the house – much like woman of old who wouldn't leave the house without lipstick on.
- Music – my taste is very mixed – I can go from top 40, hip hop and opera to Big Band Swing.

- My friends – My best friend said she loves talking to me because I always have the right response , if she is happy or has success in something, I am happy for her or whomever we are speaking about and the same if she is sad, I am sad with her and always try to help or just listen.

- Food – I love my food – I haven't always had a healthy relationship with food having experienced anorexia for a short time in my late teens and throughout my 20s, but now we are much more respectful of each other and I love baking for my family. The motto or mantra you live your life by? Since having my babies, it has been "you have pushed 2 humans out of your body, you can do anything" Now it's been changed slightly to "you have pushed 2 humans out of your body and survived breast cancer, you can do anything"!

What advice would you give to the teenage version of yourself, 18 years old and just about to embark on your life's journey?

So many things.I would say, be patient, the right one is out there for you and you WILL know when you meet him.

Don't jump in just because you're lonely. I would also tell myself to move out of home by the time I'm 20 – knowing you have to pay rent and buy food and not fail by asking your mum and dad for help is a great motivator to get your shit together.

Your figure is amazing -enjoy it, cause it's gonna change kid.

Always check a document twice before submitting – Proof read everything.

You are beautiful, don't listen to that man or let him change you, he is the damaged one, not you.

Three songs that speak to your soul?

- Led Zepplins – Black Dog
- Joan Biaz- Silver Daggers.
- Paul Kellys – From Little Things Big Things Grow

What are you most proud of yourself for and why?

My Mum said I was the best goal setter she had ever met and I grabbed that complement and I roll with that every day. An achievement starts with a thought and then a plan. I am proud that I am a goal setter, I love to have a purpose for my day, a goal set out. Even if I'm doing the same work as yesterday, I love to set myself a small goal, from baking muffins or getting up in the cold morning and going for a walk. My big goal is getting healthy to heal quickly from my re-construction and to watch my boys grow up. I would love to seem them happy and have their own children and to be an active and healthy Grandma - wow, what a trip that would be – that's the ultimate goal

Dj Dee

Who is D? What are her origins and who would you best describe her as a woman of today?

In 2020 D is a mama first and foremost, putting in every waking moment into raising a child. Who was DJ D prior to becoming a mum? A DJ/turntablist that in many cases won the title of first female to cut it up in that space, with some of those spaces being on the international tip; all whilst working a full time job, completing a couple of degrees, running a design business and an interactive company, and hosting a radio show, amongst a number of other projects. It's during sleeping hours that this mama gets to reminisce and relive her past years of cutting things up on the decks, often pulling all-nighters to put some energy back into DJ D, whilst recording my radio show/podcast '1200 Degrees Mixxbosses' – a concept that was originally broadcast in 1999 on one of the first streaming servers here in Australia. The show currently broadcasts on Wed 7-9p & Sat 8-10p on Radio2RDJ.com 88.1fm (Sydney Australia), Thursdays 7-9 on OzUrbanRadio.com 87.8fm (Perth Australia), or online anytime at 1200degrees.com.au

What is your profession? How did you end up in the Music Industry and what do you love about what you do?

I've been a teacher/head teacher since the late 90s, in tertiary education, teaching web & graphic design and its multimedia facets. I started my own design biz in the mid 90s at the age of 16 and tapped into what was then a fresh industry – the world wide web. Designing graphics and writing code by hand were all part of my daily life, with some amazing jobs that included designing & creating a number of websites for the

Australian Broadcasting Corporation, as well as later redesigning their online branding and branding applications, whilst designing/building sites for a plethora of their sub-sites which included things like ABC kids, ABC science, ABC news, Triple J and so on.

My loose plan was - work hard to save dollars to support my vinyl habit. Looking back, it is clear that all the while music was there. Growing up the story is much the same. With not many toys as a toddler, I recall playing with dad's 7 inch vinyl collection, at a time where stacking records out of their sleeves vertically in those metal or plastic racks seemed to be the trend; those beautifully coloured labels were like pieces of candy to me - I couldn't resist. This of course eventually led to me being the family's human remote control for our beloved wooden vintage entertainment unit that housed a turntable, an AM radio & one of those retro domed glass television sets – I still remember clicking the turn-dial to discover the available channels, all two or three of them lols. The next step was my own record collection that began as gifts from my older brother including a compilation entitled 'Party Songs' and 'The Muppet Show'.

The mid to late 80s is where I really started experimenting; my sister had her driver's licence and was also at her club-going peak; that meant I had access to her stereo system and tape-to-tape recorder whilst she was out. This of course meant mixtapes had to be made - yes the tedious way – hand rewind, pause, record that sample of a few seconds, next tape etc etc. Once completed, these mixes were broadcast via Dad's XD falcon, driving down Marrickville road, blasting the tape deck that we personally installed, as at the time of purchase of that particular vehicle it only came with an AM radio. It was the year of 1998 that I had my first gig - I still remember my first real feeling of crowd response, when that dance floor filled and later erupted into a balloon fight, seeing everyone in that room laughing and having a great time – for me there really was no turning back from that point. I soon progressed to my brother's hi-fi unit that included a turntable at top, having my first whirl at scratching using a 7-inch record of De La Soul's 'Say No Go' (1989), learning the do's & don'ts by feel whilst experimenting with refining sounds. I had a pen-pal at the time that had shared tapes of the Geto Boys and NWA, amongst other hip hop groups, and I was hooked!

This soon led to playing nationally at locations such as Darwin, Wollongong, Newcastle, Bowral, Melbourne, Gold Coast, Perth, Dubbo, Cairns, Brisbane, Sunshine Coast, Albury, and Terrigal. Each set I did always started with a custom intro featuring various elements of turntablism, and before I knew it I was club gigging every weekend, and jet setting every other. With a strong online presence that led to international bookings from over 35 countries, I often had to knock back offers due to work commitments, though a few trips were undertaken when events fell during school vacation periods. These included the Middle East in 2004, the Czech Republic in 2006 & 2007, Malaysia in 2008 & 2009 respectively. Additionally, those DMC goals were achieved in 2005 when I placed 8th in Australia, as the only female competitor, in the national DMC Championships that were held in Melbourne. I later placed 3rd in NSW in 2015, once again as the only female competitor.

You are a woman of many talents and skills which is something that is so admired and inspirational to others. As Australia's premier HipHop Turntablist, you have taken the art of djing to a new level, with your attention to detail and the highest

respect for the craft of turntablism. You have been a club / tour and radio DJ for the better part of 2 decades and have represented female DJs from the very start. Now, as a wife and mother to your adorable son you still share your love of turntablism through your radio show and various teaching opportunities. How do you find the balance of motherhood and your own personal evolution to make life work for you?

I think that was perhaps the hardest thing for me – to go from maximum speed to zero. I was so used to working a full time job that demanded much overtime, running 2 businesses, hosting my weekly radio show, helping out at the radio station as production coordinator & programming committee member, running mix bosses and all its entities including our online 24-7 radio station, DJing at various clubs nationally/internationally, supporting international artists on tour and creating mixtapes, restoring my 1964 Chevy ragtop, and so the list went on – to then slam on the brakes in an instant and shift focus to 100% on raising a child was an extreme change to say the least, though perhaps much needed and without a doubt the most rewarding and amazing. To see this child only a few weeks old dancing to classic rnb & hip hop artists, I already knew we shared a love for music. To see him respond to songs in certain ways, like he knew those songs, though I knew I'd never played them to him; it made me think back and realize that he must have heard these tracks when in the womb! We made it our daily task (and still do) to play some dope tunes and dance together most every day, and yes I have saved a number of video recordings that I'll be sure to share at his 21st lols.

Fast forward a few years to today and yes it's still a mission, though I get all my tasks done nocturnally – yes late or all-nighters is the only way I can really get things completed without interruption. Even then there's often the 'mummy where are you' or late night scream with an adorable child standing at the doorway rubbing his eyes; many a time this has led to mama pretend sleeping to get child down, only to wake up at 8 or 9am the next morning with turntables still spinning and laptop still recording.

What do you think are the most important characteristics when it comes to creating a life on your terms and at times going against the usual stereotypes of life?

Determination, perseverance, dedication & knowing what you want – eye on the prize, though don't forget to enjoy that journey as half or maybe even most of the fun is in getting there I can say that in my earlier days I went against the grain on a few occasions – my traditional European parents saying that playing in clubs in the am hours was no place for a girl; securing national bookings under my gender neutral name 'DJ D' only to get cancellations once they found out it was a female; to walking across dancefloors with record crates when people were not accustomed to seeing female deejays in the urban/rnb hip hop scene, and hearing patrons say 'what's she gonna do???' Looking back it almost became my mission to turn these things around, I put my head down and worked hard at my craft that then led to – overhearing my father proudly sharing with his peers the hourly rate I was getting plus the international bookings that were coming through; fate would have that cancelling promoter see me play at a high profile event and after only 1.5 songs come over shake my hand and say he was flying me to his city to play an event;

and those patrons? I was grateful to have worked on my skills to the point where I hopped on the decks and just started cutting – you should have seen their mouths drop - 'wow I ain't ever seen a girl cut that fast' lols. Practice and dedication really do pay off in the long run.

As a woman of creativity, passion, strength, ambition and determination, how would you best describe what success means to you and do you feel you have achieved success in your life?

To me success equals achievement, setting out to achieve something and completing that task to the best of one's ability. I recall a promoter back in the early 2000s asking me, whilst we were at an interstate show, why I didn't have a team behind me to push me further in the public eye. I still remember the surprised look on his face when I said that I was content and really happy with what I had achieved – that look was like 'huh? Don't you want more?' Although there are still one or two items on that wish list of goals, I was super grateful and content having achieved almost everything I had set out to do at such an early age. That being said, this is not something that will ever end for me – my love of music and hitting those turntables will always be a part of my lifestyle. Additional notable achievements include supporting artists that I had grown up listening to – to be able to do this has been an absolute dream come true. Artists have included Ricky Bell (Bell Biv Devoe/New Edition), Naughty By Nature, Kci & Jojo (Jodeci), Montell Jordan, Horace Brown, Tank, Blackstreet, 112, DJ Jam (Snoop Dogg & Dr Dre's DJ) and a handful of others. More recently, it's been an absolute honour to host international artists in my 64 impala #StraightOuttaTha64, once again artists that I grew up listening to. These have included Xzibit, King Quez (Outlawz), Chauncey Black (Blackstreet), Tha Alkaholiks, DJ Yella (NWA), Curtis young (Dr Dre's son), Baby Eazy E (Eazy E's son), Spice 1, Freedom Williams (C&C Music Factory), Ty Dolla Sign, and Masta Ace (Crooklyn Dodgers) amongst others. Moments like these have always made me think that it's more like 2 or 3 degrees of separation, not 6.

What are the 5 things you cannot live without and why?

1. The number one slot has to go to my son who will forever be my number one. I recall the first 'comeback' gig I did which was during daylight hours. Having no extra hands here I had arranged

to drop him off at his grandparents place for the first time which was roughly an hour drive, from there I would drive one and a half hours to the gig destination. It was one of the hottest days and I remember melting as I finally pulled into a parking spot. I called the grandparents house to check up on things and my little guy gets on the phone saying: 'mummy where are you, you have been gone a long time, come back'. Even though I was running on about 3 hrs sleep in 2 days putting together this trickset, I nearly found myself saying 'bugger the gig' lols, and starting up that engine.

2. My music and headphones have always been with or near me. As a child that got car sick my Walkman and cassette tape was my medicine. As a DJ in flight for national and international gigs that also felt uneasy on planes, my ipod and DJ headphones were once again my anti-nausea fix. As a mama birthing her first almost 10pound child, my ipod and DJ headphones were my pain relief; the midwife chuckling as I had one hand in the air with eyes closed on the bouncy birthing ball whilst listening to Big L, with Xzibit joining

me in the emergency theatre for the actual birthing (still super grateful to the midwife that made that happen).

3. My Vinyl and 1200s have to enter on this list, with these turntables having been with me since the late 90s, and vinyl since my early childhood, not to mention my fathers 7" collection that goes back to purchases from the 1950s. When asked if I was having a second child I would often respond with 'that room' pointing to the room of turntables, vinyl and other DJ matter, 'aint going no-where' lols.

4. With all my late-nighters I point blank refuse to survive without Tea/Coffee - I'm almost sure it is the main matter that runs within these veins ;p.

5. Finally, my first baby - my 64 Impala. This car was a dream of mine since my early teens, I knew what I wanted – a 1964 Chevrolet Impala convertible, candy apple red with white interior. My mother knew of my dream and would often point out cadillacs and other classic vehicles saying 'dream baby dream'. For years we searched high and low, with 2 or 3 deals falling through. Until a dear friend put me in touch with a contact in the US

who was selling his – it was white with a red interior though the rest fit the description of the dream ride. We agreed on a price, did the virtual handshake, and let the dramas of getting this car to Australia unfold (I'll save those stories for another time, tho let me tell you I could near write a book on this process alone lols). It was at least 6 months later that I first laid eyes on her in person! Somewhere in the middle of this story my mother had passed, originally being a cancer survivor though later succumbing to this disease. You can imagine my tears when I opened the original booklet from 1964 only to find that the date of delivery of this car to its first owner in 1964 was the same date my mother had passed in 2010. So, to this day, I always say she rides with me 100.

The motto or mantra you live your life by?

Well the one I am most known for I coined back in around the year 2000 – 'Scratch as if no one is watching' lols.

What advice would you give to the teenage version of yourself, 18 years old and just about to embark on your life's journey?

Not to worry so much about what others think. Sure, it didn't really hold me back too much, though in my early days, negative comments did stick. It almost became my mission to turn these people around, and funnily enough, some of these people later became my number one followers. Perhaps the most memorable moment that supports this advice was having performed support at the Montell Jordan This is how we do it tour in 2005. We had just rocked the Kci & Jojo Jodeci tour the year before and were all prepped to do this next show when I was told last minute that I wasn't permitted to use the people I had arranged.

With some very last minute planning we pulled it off, though I remember being super disappointed with the performance; things just hadn't run to plan - the stage was bouncy, the turntables weren't reinforced so that meant constant skippage, amongst other performance dramas. I put that video tape aside not having watched it in full, and only mustered up the courage to watch it again 15 years later. Watching it back now I was like 'hey, this ain't too bad at all' lols. Hearing what I had thought were people in the audience making negative comments, later in the tape turned to praising my track selection and reminiscing about the tracks I was playing, saying how good they were – all those years and I was wishing I had watched that video tape in full 15 years earlier.

Three songs that speak to your soul?

I'm going to bend the rules a little and include the original samples as well:

- De La Soul – Me Myself & I (1989)
- Funkadelic – Knee Deep (1979)
- DJ Jazzy Jeff & The Fresh Prince – Live at Union Square (1988)
- Cheryl Lynn – Got To Be Real (1978)
- Herman Kelly & Life – Dance to The Drummers Beat (1978)
- Dr Dre – Let Me Ride (1992)
- Parliament – Mothership Connection (1975).

What are you most proud of yourself for and why?

In short, really just to have achieved what I had set out to achieve, nothing beats that sense of accomplishment and satisfaction. Proud to have represented for the ladies wherever possible in what was traditionally a male dominated industry.

Eden Dessalegn

Who is Eden Dessalegn? What are her origins and who would you best describe her as a woman of today?

Eden is an Ethiopian born, Australian raised, 32 year old woman. An entrepreneur, mother to my gorgeous son and blessing "Kingston", a positive contributor to the world, a dancer, a lover of life, passionate about achieving anything I set my mind to, travel, family, friends and thrive from creating happiness for others.

What is your profession and how did you start your journey in the hair and beauty Industry?

I am a Hairstylist (specialising in hair braiding) and a business owner. I began my journey when I was 13 years old, it was around the time when my parents went through a divorce. I grew up with very coarse thick and curly afro hair which my mother used to help wit, at that time life was difficult for my mother, she had an unsuccessful restaurant business, a car accident, had an abortion, and dealing with the divorce which left mum in debt due to my dads gambling addiction. Mum had to work really hard even doing night shift for about 2 years to pay the mortgage and raise me. I had to learn how to do my own hair and braids was the best option as it was long lasting and a protective style. Mum would bring back hair braiding posters from Ethiopia and I would try to copy the styles I didn't have YouTube or social media, I would just try and recreate what I saw. I practiced on myself and everyone at school. I braided hair all throughout high school. I would charge $5- $20 and book appointments in the library, during lunch time, and after school. After high school I used my hobby as my side hustle while I worked in the corporate field until I began setting up stalls at markets and festivals which led me to my first Easter show to then the opening of my studio Eden Stylz.

You are a woman of many talents and skills which is something that is so admired and inspirational to others. Out of all of your creative talent, be it a dancer, hair braiding connoisseur and just a lover of life in general, how does Eden Dessalegn survive and thrive through them all?

Thank you kindly for that lovely compliment. I honestly chase what makes me happy. I'm a planner, I like to organise and plan ahead and always have a plan A and B but I'm always open to changes and things going in a different direction as I believe everything happens for a reason. I'm a firm believer in balance. I feel that a well rounded life is a full life, work hard, play hard.

What do you think are the most important characteristics when it comes to creating a life on your terms and at times going against the usual stereotypes of life?

The most important attributes that assisted in creating my life is believing in myself, taking calculated risks, not being afraid to work hard, being true to myself and following my passion and what makes me happy, being resilient, honest and kind. For years I believed you had to follow "society's rules" go to school, get a job and work for someone, but no one told me that I can create a life that suited me where work doesn't feel like work and holidays aren't to escape life, to live life to the fullest every day.

As a woman of passion, strength, ambition and loyalty, how would you best describe what success means to you and do you feel you have achieved success in your life?

Success to me is a clear conscious, sleeping peacefully without a heavy burden, not necessarily tangible. I also believe success is an ongoing thing, a journey not a destination and most importantly happiness.For many years I felt that I wasn't able to reach it as I was working so hard but wasn't seeing results, I set myself a 5 year goal at the age of 25 which I achieved all at 30 years old. That's actually the first time I felt success, but the moment I feel it most is when I can make someone else happy.

What are the 5 things you cannot live without and why?

I can not live without my :

- Mum- she is my rock, my everything, who loves me unconditionally and the only person in the world who would give their life to me. We are each others keeper. best friend and support.

- My son - My pride and joy, by heart and soul and daily joy.

- My friends - I have 2 groups of girl friends with many years of friendship (10- 21 years of friendship) they are my supporters, there for me, encouraging. They are who I vent to, party with and create memories with. Real friendships are important in life and say alot about an individual's character by the friendships they hold.

- Music- allows me to dance which brings me joy

- Food- well that's life! It brings people together, nourishes the body and who's able to live without food lol.(one more)

- Laughter- I love to surround myself with those who make me laugh because it just feels good.

The motto or mantra you live your life by?

I have a tattoo on my back which reads " Live the life you love, Love the life you live" by Bob Marley. I believe in this and will be something I will pass on to my son. Another one would be "Don't live life by default, Live life by design" .... simple but powerful quotes which help shape my life.

What advice would you give to the teenage version of yourself, 18 years old and just about to embark on your life's journey?

Growing up I struggled a lot with weight and body shaming myself. I never loved how I looked, being in the dance industry at a young age and being surrounded by thin people I felt as if I was permanently on a diet to fit in. Until I travelled the world and gained confidence with how I looked. I would say be kind to yourself and love the body you're in. Otherwise I wouldn't change a thing as everything that happened in my life was meant to happen as it led me to where I am now.

Three songs that speak to your soul?

1. Alicia keys - Superwoman
2. Destiny's child - Independent Women
3. Chaka Khan - I'm every woman

What are you most proud of yourself for and why?

- Dancing in a Hollywood movie
- Completing a Masters degree
- Running my own business and opening a salon
- Doing what makes me and others happy every day
- Travelling the world
- Purchasing my dream car
- Purchasing my own property
- Most proud ....being a mum!

Most of these were in my five-year goal, 90% didn't go as planned but God also had his plans for me. I'm proud that no matter what I went through, lost friendships, broken relationships, financial losses, lack of father figure, I was persistent, driven and determined to never give up. If you do good, good things happen. Even though I have done quite a bit I know there is still so much more to come and I have so much more to do.

I count my blessings on the daily and strive to constantly be the best version of myself, to leave a legacy and to be someone my son will be proud of.

Pamela Diaz

Who is Pamela? What are your origins and how would you best describe her as a woman of today?

My name is Pamela. I was born and raised in Sydney's Inner West, and I'm the only child of migrant parents from Chile, who arrived in Sydney in 1970. Both my parents worked full-time; Mum worked in a shoe factory as a shoe designer and Dad worked in computers. My Mum was always polite and social, whilst Dad is analytical. I think I carry these attributes with me today. My childhood was fun and I of course I got up to mischief; riding my bike around the neighbourhood, hanging out with my neighbours and friends and it's these memories that I hold so very dear to me. Growing up in my hood made me appreciate the melting pot Sydney is. I loved visiting my friends houses – they were Italian, Greek, Lebanese Egyptian and Croatian backgrounds – and it enabled me to appreciate cultures, traditions, language, respect and I could identify myself with so many.

Throughout my teen years, my parents always encouraged me to do my best. I learnt to be resourceful with what I had and not to go beyond my means. These principals are still within me today. I didn't really like being an only child, but I learned to love my own company. As a child, I didn't like my name (sorry Mum), and at one point, I wanted to change it. I didn't have a back-up name so I was stuck with the one given to me. In the last decade, I've learnt to love my name and I hear myself introduce myself as Pamela as I extend my hand to greet someone new. Funny. I don't know why, but as a kid I struggled with my identity and that weird awkwardness. Where did I fit in? Am I an Aussie or classified as Other?

I'm pretty lucky to know my entire family – both in Sydney and Santiago. The first time I travelled to Santiago I was 4, and it was via Disneyland. Oh how I loved Disneyland. I have fond memories of my grandparents' homes. The buzz of activity with family around, the simple kitchen with its electric stove cluttered with its rustic pots and pans, the natural Andean country landscapes and overabundant vineyards you see when you're travelling in the bus to get there, the random kisses and love poured into the cuddles family member gave. It was the curiosity as a child and seeing things for the first time, which was so special. The women in my family are strong with an infectious joy in all they do. Always a smile on their face. I strive for that.

I've always had an interest in my family's history and wanted to learn their stories. My Mother's side, I know well and everyone in it. My great grandparents Jose and Rosa migrated from Asyria (modern day Iran) to Santiago in 1930 to escape war. I didn't know much about my father's side of the family other than the occasional story, but lucky to know them and have my father's grandmother. With Mum and Dad being my first teachers, my influencers and they always taught me about love and respect for others. I'd like to think that I still carry that with me today. My late Mother always said "Be like a lady" and I hear her voice echo as I told my daughter. I love my brown skin and the fact that I don't look like everyone else. I am proud of my heritage. I care about the family values and traditions we have, and teaching my child so she can continue them and make them her own. I am independent, confident with who I am and learned to go with the flow. I've learned to accept myself for who I am and let go of what others think. The fun is in the growth and the journey. I'm still evolving.

What is your profession? How did you end up in the industry you are in and what do you love about what you do?

I studied Hospitality because I wanted to travel and loved the idea of cheap flights (I mean, who doesn't?). Turns out all I took away was typing skills. I was in the top 5. My career started with a little bit of help. I'm second generation IBM. I was accepting a role at Deakin University for an Assistant when I received a phone call from IBM Australia saying I too was accepted for a PA position. It was a tough decision for me to make where to work. I felt conflicted - Do I do pursue something on my own and in my own way, or, do I take a great opportunity despite the help? I ended up taking the help.

My Manager had a great leadership team, and with any leadership team, you have a mixed bag of personalities. With my Desktop services, IT helpdesk, corporate knowledge, "everyone is a customer" philosophy, I took my skills and principles and applied them everywhere I went and developed them along the way. I travelled to Europe and did the expat thing. In London I started temping as a PA/Office Assistant working for some pretty exciting companies as I wasn't confident enough to go for roles in IT. Eventually, I bit the bullet and I started contracting in the IT industry. This was a time where I had put everything I had learnt into practise and I surprised myself with my abilities.

I had to be confident in myself no matter what. I was accountable for me and had no one to lean on. I was my own Boss now. Travelling was now part of the job and I loved every minute of it. Sure, it was hard work (early and late starts) but I got to see and experience cities I wouldn't have even thought of visiting. When I returned home to Sydney, again I had to learn my worth, value and my skill set. I was given another opportunity. Grateful for the faith, I took on the role which would enable me to travel around Asia Pacific and even a gig for a Latin America office which I had to travel to Venezuela and Mexico, all thanks to my language and technical skills. See, language does help!! Recovering from illness I had to get back into the workforce. It was difficult for me to be mobile as I was challenged physically.

I thought of what could I possibly do to use my skills and knowledge and somewhere that wouldn't be far from home. I ended up in Real Estate. I was an office Manager/assistant for three years. I thank my Manager for taking a chance on me as well as loved working with the team he had built. When I started I was on crutches and a walking stick. I wasn't confident in my physical capabilities. Three years later with determination and goals, I made the hard decision to leave and returned to the corporate world and loving it. You never stop learning. Period.

At the core of everything you do, you have a fighter's spirit that has seen you through incredible challenges both physically and emotionally. Becoming a mother to your beautiful daughter also

brought about the huge obstacle of cancer to overcome whilst trying to care for your newborn. You are a survivor with a fierce love for life and your family above and beyond. Can you put into words how you have been able to balance the challenges of motherhood and your own physical and personal evolution to make life work for you?

Sometimes you don't know how far you've come until you look back. I've got to be honest and I don't really like talking about this part of my life. It's a significant piece of who I am today, however, diving down deep in my emotional repressed dark corners, where we go....

I should mention that during the time I'm writing this, it marks nine years since it happened. I can't help but get emotional this time of year. Ok, so at this stage of my life, it was bitter sweet. Career was good, I was married to someone I had been with for a long time, I had just turned 37 and was expecting my first baby. What could go wrong? A few weeks leading up to my baby's due date, I felt there was a problem on the right side of my body - specifically my pelvis and leg. Upon going to weekly hospital visits, I was told that it was my body preparing for the baby and my pelvis was taped up as it became 'unaligned' (whatever that meant). After a massage and taping, they gave me a walking stick to help me walk around. Having no idea what that meant, I just sucked it up and continued on.

When on maternity leave, as my baby was moving more and I was preparing for her arrival, my right side became painful. It was hard to walk and put pressure on my foot. I stayed a lot of the time at my parents' house to help me as I was comfortable with surroundings. The pain was getting worse and I remember I couldn't walk to the bathroom from the lounge room. All 15 steps and I had to hold onto the walls for support. One of our neighbours happened to be a physiotherapist so I went to visit her for massages. As I couldn't walk properly she gave me a mobility frame with wheels. Crazy! It's now a week before my due date, and during my weekly hospital visit, my Mum drove me to the hospital and she left me at the front as she had to look for parking. I couldn't walk. The pain was excruciating.

When in my appointment I told the nurses that I couldn't carry my baby anymore and I needed her to be delivered. Like, this week. Now, we all know that women have a high level of pain threshold but this was ridiculous. With my Mum by my side, and after some demonstration, the nurses asked for an OB to come and see me. I had told him what I was experiencing and we agreed that I was to deliver my baby by caesarean. She was to be delivered the following week. I have never experienced love until the moment I saw my baby girl, and I promised her that I would never let anything happen to her.

The following morning, still besotted with my newborn, my right leg didn't feel quite right. It just felt 'weird'. I was sent to bed rest and when it came time for me to get up from the hospital bed to walk around, I asked the nurse for my walking stick. "No Love, you won't need it."

With one step on my right leg, I face planted to the floor. The nurse hit the panic button and I've never seen so many nurses around me. I was put back in bed and a series of tests began. Four days after my daughter was born, I was diagnosed with a rare bone cancer known as Osteosarcoma. This cancer is normally found in children, young adults and dogs. Not in middle aged women.

I was transferred to RPA Hospital (Sydney) by ambulance to start my treatment. I was a new Mum and now I'm a cancer patient. How did this happen? Are you sure? What was supposed to be a moment of my life where it was to be happy, joyful and celebrated, instead was darkened by this unwanted chaos and unbelievable emotions. This was not the experience I signed up for. My Dad was my rock. I have no idea how he kept on seeing the positive side of things. He just did. He got me though so much. He was my constant. He always says "We have a problem. We have to fix it." And that he did.

My Mum focused on looking after the baby, and she fell into a deep depression. I can understand now, as a mother. No one wants to see their child sick or weak. It was such a dark period of my life. As the cancer was quite aggressive, I had three rounds of heavy chemo and after each session, I was an in-patient as my body couldn't cope. It was starting to shut down.

One night in July 2011 It was about 2:30am and I couldn't sleep. I was still yet to have my first surgery and I was so very anxious. I went to go wash my hands from the bathroom, and I remember looking up into the mirror. I had no hair, no eyebrows, and no eyelashes. Not a single hair on my body. I had never felt so naked, vulnerable or scared in my life. "Who are you?" I didn't recognise myself. I certainly didn't see Me in the mirror. I was so angry that all this had happened. But I was determined to get this cancer out so I can pick up my life where I left off. My goal was to simply go home and spend time with my baby. That's it.

Surgery meant stripping back my muscles in my pelvis, removing a quarter of my pelvic bone to give it a dose of radiation, then reattaching it with bolts and screws. Recovery meant... 12 weeks of bed rest. No movement whatsoever. Weight loss plan to the extreme. Jenny Craig, eat your heart out! Overall my daughter was my reason to get better. I had to get better. I wanted to go home. I had been waiting for her so long.

During my 12 week bed rest, my goal was to simply take my daughter out for a walk around the block. That's all I wanted. And I did. Don't tell me I can't! Since October 2011, I've had three other surgeries. I have a titanium pelvis and a full hip replacement. No more chemo, even though I should have follow-up rounds. I give thanks to my remarkable surgeon. He continues to do radical surgery and I am grateful for being one of his subjects. I help him out for ongoing research. I'm trying my best to take it to the next level with my daughter. Sharing wonderful experiences like what I had as a child and trying to make things as normal as possible i.e. travel, show her this beautiful city of ours, to be proud of her family and where they came from, appreciate the sacrifices they had to experience and overcome.

My new normal. It's discipline. I push myself. I try to balance everything. I don't have a formula. I try not to sweat the small stuff. My daughter saved me and I thank God that I have her, every day.

What do you think are the most important characteristics when it comes to creating a life on your terms and at times going against the usual stereotypes of life?

I guess it depends on your definition of 'stereotypes'?I had my daughter at 37, and for some that's considered late in life. But for me it was the right time. There were so many things I wanted to do before settling down. If I was going to bring a child into this world, I needed to know who I am and what I stand for so I can teach them along the way.

As a single mum you can only do the best you can. You can't be both a mother and father. They're two different roles where you learn two sets of values to make you one person. I believe you can only lead by example and hopefully they pick up things along the way. Perfection is exhausting. I can only be me, and do me, and show that you can be yourself and show all emotions as we cannot always keep it together. There's always a breaking point.

Loving yourself and showing that high vibration. Showing people who you are and not hiding behind words (or a keyboard). I remember my humble beginnings and I'm not about to be ashamed or hide it. If you're lucky, you get to experience and enjoy 70 birthdays, 70 summers, 70 springs, 70 autumns, 70 winters. You have to embrace all that comes your way. There's a bigger reason beyond control. I'm lucky enough to have a strong group of women I call friends. Together we encourage each other and have each other's backs. We're doing things our way now, with influences from our mothers. And my daughter has these women in her life too. Great role models. The best any girl can have.

As a woman of creativity, passion, strength, ambition and determination, how would you best describe what success means to you and do you feel you have achieved success in your life?

To some, success is measured by the amount of money you have in the bank, the car you drive or the house you live in. I define success as following your passion. I base it on what I have achieved, my surroundings and hitting those small goals that make you become the person you are. I think it's also the result of a lesson you've learned, the feeling of happiness you get within yourself from providing a contribution or participation in.

A little while back, I wrote a list of my own achievements to remind myself how far I've come and to show how I have evolved as a person. It's easy to forget what you've done in life. I think everyone has got to acknowledge their success in their own right. Sometimes I think we can be hard on ourselves, again, I think that comes down to one's definition of 'successes'. Our kids are also our success.

What are the things you cannot live without and why?

1. Family and Friends - Family and friends is the glue of who I am today. They know who I am and accept me – all of me.

2. Music - As LL Cool J said "I can't live without my radio". Sister Sledge said "We're lost in music. We're caught in a trap". So true for me when I hear

a beat. Music enables you to feel so many emotions. To express yourself.

3. Camera - Again, something else to capture a moment in time, to hold memories.

4. Ocean - It's amazing as I'm an air sign but love the water. Growing up in Australia means you're surrounded by it. The weightless feeling when you float. It's a new world to explore when you snorkel. It's my escape. My happy place.

The motto or mantra you live your life by?

There are so many. If you don't ask, you don't get. Don't tell me I can't. It's not what you know, it's who you know.

What advice would you give to the teenage version of yourself, 18 years old and just about to embark on your life's journey?

- Be patient, don't settle. You deserve the best so don't take the first offer of anything that comes your way.

- Don't sweat the small stuff and you know what's important.

- Forget the 'haters' and start worrying about yourself.

- Let go of the perfection as you already are. Let go of the expectations that you think are there, because they're not.

- Trust your instincts. That gut feeling is real so you make your own decisions and you do what's best for you.

- You are gorgeous, and you are enough. Love your curves.

- If people cannot accept you for who you are then they're not worth your time. It's ok to be on your own. And you get better with age!

- You are funny, loving, worth, strong and confident. You're a unicorn! You're an amazing catch!

- Have savings plan and stick to it. You don't need all that money at this age. Save it – you'll thank me later. Salary sacrifice - our Superannuation will thank us!!

Three songs that speak to my soul?

Song 1 - Vivir Mi Vida by Mark Anthony, 2013 (Latino)

Song 2 - Finally by Kings of Tomorrow feat Julie McKnight, 2001 (House)

Song 3 - Anything by Sade (RnB / Soul / Jazz)

What are you most proud of yourself for and why?

More than ever, I'm proud of the attitude I have towards life and those in it. The last ten years have been the most challenging I've had. I could easily have fallen in a very dark space full of negativity, resentment and consumed by self-pity. But I choose not to.

I mean,

- I was ill for a long time (2011)
- I got made redundant (2012)
- I missed out on my normal life
- My marriage fell apart (2013)
- My mother passed away (2018)
- This year my Aunt passed away (2020)
- But the sun always comes out after the rain...

- I've survived cancer and I get to tell the story
- I've found another job and I enjoy it
- I'm making my new normal
- I have a great relationship with myself
- I try to lead by example with what my mother taught me
- To be the caring Aunt to my nieces and nephews how my aunt was with me.

Sure, I could be more in tune with myself. I actually asked my daughter this question. Her answer…You're loving and strong, Mama!

Weave Dibden Neck

Who is Weave? What are her origins and who would you best describe her as a woman of today?

Answering a question like this is not always as easy as we imagine, as it is supposed to be the simplest thing, knowing who we are...but I have learned over the many years that the evolving identity is one of many challenges. I think that living in the current climate as we are right now, I feel like the identity of a strong, independent, free thinking woman that I am , has had to conform in a most unusual way. I set up my life to be free, to work for myself, take care of my baby, have the ability to arise at any moment, watch every sunset I wanted to watch. Living through something like covid 19 has taken these privileges away, so we now have to look at ourselves in a completely different manner. How do we find our resolve in a time like this, who are we and how do we handle something like this when you are a free bird? I think this is when we can really discover the answers to these questions. Who am I,how do I manage my emotions and well being and career and opportunities when your freedoms are taken.

I've discovered a beautiful sense of self and ability to let go, that was something I havnt been able to do before. So I think if you asked me this question a few months ago, I would have given my standard answers of , I am WEAVE, I am determined and focussed and loyal and nothing can deter me from my path and I will suffer in silence to find my dream goals. I think now that i have learnt how to actually understand that everything is so much bigger and that we really have a vulnerable place on this earth. I think my answer is now, I am WEAVE, I am strong, independent, malleable , forgiving, have the ability to accept change and I realise that whatever I do , wherever i am , I am just as me with a greater sense of responsibility to the greater cause. My footprint, my decision making process comes with greater value now. What I say is important. We are all very deeply, incredibly, beautifully important.

I grew up on a beautiful thoroughbred breeding stable in the gorgeous Mount Lofty Ranges of the Adelaide Hills in South Australia. It truly was a beautiful environment with horse riding a part of my every day, dad was a chairman of a race course so entertaining international guests was a regular part of our childhoods, so I think I just was obsessed with the idea of dressing up and being the seventies, it was such a fabulous time for fashion! Mum was very beautiful and very glamorous so I think I got my love for it during these times. There was also a lady in the main street of Oakbank that we used to ride our ponies down to visit. She was called the Oakbank Weaver. I was obsessed with her stories of buying vans and driving around international countries making weavings and collecting art and bringing them back to our little town. I figured we had a deep connection being our names were the same!

After a family break up we left that lifestyle behind and was quite impressionable I would say to the big wide new world. I then discovered hip hop.

Some fellas from London had arrived in Adelaide and I gotta watch them break in the main mall of the city and Ice T had come to town, and LL cool J was my hero, and I started making bomber jackets at the age of 14 out of old bubble skirts to make a bit of money on the sly!!! My first label. All of this really describes the versatility of the woman that I have become today

What is your profession? How did you end up in the Fashion industry and what do you love about what you do?

I have been so blessed to have always known what I wanted to do, outside of wanting to be a professional horse rider , then truck driver, I then found fashion! I was blessed to have been given the gift of independence, So I was able to navigate my path without being dictated to. I took off to Sydney at 17 after being accepted into the most prestigious fashion school in Australia at the time, and took off by myself with 150 dollars in my pocket and a friends aunty to stay with until I found a house! This schooling at East Sydney was the pinnacle to learning the ins and outs of the industry on a creative level and pursue my label I was working on. I worked for a couple of different people on the side and nightclub doors as we do to get by, but remained completely independent once I left the fashion school. I was still heavily into Hip hop at this stage and I met my partner of the time whom we had a beautiful daughter and started the street wear label 'Cyberthief'. It was quite a unique thing at the time, the internet had just blown up and I had these amazing friends, Paul and Pablo, that showed me how to work it, they built me an amazing site that integrated fashion, music and art, where local graf artists could submit their work, rappers with songs, photos etc, and it became a beautiful voice of an underground generation of the time. It was fairly short lived but it was a fantastic integration of clothing, art , music, dance. Headquarters were at an amazing warehouse in Surry hills where we had parties, sales and installations for the label. It was a wonderful time and I was able to be there with my daughter to watch her soak up all the artistic energy around.

I guess after a while I started to grow up a little , as did some of the artists I was dressing, so weddings, red carpets etc became more of the requested attire. I evolved into more of a tailor (which I had been trained in in Adelaide already) and started to develop a different approach to the design philosophy I was working under.

I started to enjoy high fashion alot more and realised that my potential was so much greater if I could break the chains of being just subject to one genre. Creatively it opened my eyes and capabilities and techniques to a much wider audience and I loved it.

You are a woman of many talents and skills which is something that is so admired and inspirational to others. You have been a respected fashion designer for many years now, winning over local and international clients and celebrities with your beautiful bridal and couture designs handcrafted by yourself. Your company ByWeave has been a heart filled project for you and seeing your works grace global Fashion Week catwalks gaining critical acclaim and respect from your peers. At the heart of it all you are a woman who loves her humble Sydney roots, living by the ocean and being mum to your beautiful daughter. How would you explain what the balance between running a successful fashion label and your own personal evolution as a woman has been like?

Well firstly I think success is in the eye of the beholder ! I have been through many tough times and many peaks, which definitely has taught me to realise the fragility of running your own business. I think that once I took the pressure off myself to be a success in the eyes of others, it really helped me maintain the balance. For me, success is raising a healthy and happy child, which I have done, and maintaining a business throughout this is probably one of the biggest achievements of my life! I actually in my heart believe you cannot do EVERYTHING brilliantly. Something generally has to give. I know the times I put my business first were the times I saw my daughter need me the most, so you have to juggle that and rearrange that to make sure the family doesn't suffer because of it. I've had some incredible experiences, yes , like showing internationally, which to be honest, is one of my greatest achievements as a designer. There isn't a thrill I have felt before more than watching my own show, I get tingles thinking about it! The work, the dedication, the management of it all, it's so thrilling with such an incredible pay off after. That may not always be financial, but it certainly is a highlight of a career and makes you realise you can achieve anything. Such a powerful way to connect with your audience and push yourself in the most personal of ways. Being exposed like that is something that you have to be so able to accept the criticism as well as the accolade. Because believe me it comes, in all sorts of ways in the fashion industry! I have certainly toughened up as a woman because of it and the evolution of me throughout this process has been nothing short of powerful.

What do you think are the most important characteristics when it comes to creating a life on your terms and at times going against the usual stereotypes of life?

BEING BRAVE! There is nothing more I can say!!! HAHA ! You have to be so brave to fight through so many hurdles and to not be scared of an outcome that may not have been on the spreadsheet! I think ultimately there are two choices, as Shakespear said, 'to be or not to be' ! We have the ability to navigate our own path and accept life is there to be taken, but you have to be available to the possibilities of failure, and be able to get right back up on that horse when it does. To me failure in a task, may be just that the visualised outcome is not as originally perceived, so we can decide to sink into the idea of failure, or we use that experience of one of positivity, how do we do better next time, how do we change our way' to experience a different outcome. I actually have issues with the word failure, being it can rearrange the way we do things for a better next time and it becomes knowledge instead.

As a woman of passion, strength, loyalty and compassion, how would you best describe what success means to you and do you feel you have achieved success in your life?

I have absolutely achieved success in my life, when we perceive success as being happy, strong, free and stable. I have a wonderful selection of incredible people around me, I have the ability to make change, I have a strong voice, I have been able to do what I love every single day, I have been able to raise a health happy child that will continue on the idea of strong independent women, and I am loved.

I feel incredibly blessed that my work has given me the opportunity to travel the world, and to meet amazing people that also do amazing things. With my heart heavily involved in the music industry, dressing and creating for musicians, singers, bands, came incredibly naturally to me. Creating outside of my norm, being the collections, creating for these creatives, and also tv video, gave me an opening to push myself, and enjoy closely the talents of others in that working relationship, which often grew into personal relationships. My best friend came from our mutual love of music when we were young and to this day we remain as thick as thieves. I also create wedding gowns, and more often than not I become very close with my brides. I have very long standing relationships with these people which is a true measure of success in my eyes. Respect, loyalty and independence.

What are the 5 things you cannot live without and why?

- My daughter Chaquira, because she is my heartbeat ,

- My cat nala, because I innately need something to care for now my daughter has moved out ! And the purring of her when I put her on my heart engages in complete peace,

- Pencils and paper (that rolls into one!) because without these tools the imagery in my brain isnt translated into a working piece. There are technical things that need to be worked out from the initial vision to the working object, how to make it functional, so I love the process of putting it down on paper to see vision to reality.

- Nature, I live very close to the ocean and forest and this again brings me complete peace, and a perspective on why we as a technological age must reconsider how we operate.

- Fabric. I actually get a physical reaction in my belly when I fall in love with a fabric. The love I have for what I do is like I didn't choose it, it chose me. I feel I was blessed with a unique gift, and I do not take that for granted. Some people say I'm so lucky to have known what i wanted to do at such a young age. I agree, I feel incredibly lucky for that, the rest can only come with pure determination and very hard work, but the seed was planted from spirits above Im sure!!!

The motto or mantra you live your life by?

'Love many , Trust few , and always row your own canoe'. I actually in fact bought a beautiful wooden canoe because this mantra has sunk from deep within and I knew I needed to bring it alive!

What advice would you give to the teenage version of yourself, 18 years old and just about to embark on your life's journey?

'You got this kid'.

One thing I've learned about being in business, is there are many people that will try to stunt your growth. Whether for personal reasons, or other reasons, you must stand your ground, fight for what you believe in, be completely true to yourself and push on through. Every step is one in the right direction, we must listen to those that offer positive advice and feedback, listen to those that give more criticism, all of it to be analysed and put in your thinking cap. We can find lessons in all sorts of amazing places. There are so many ups and downs in life, business, creativity, all of it matters. Tomorrow is always another day, so never stop believing.

Three songs that speak to your soul?

1. Bob Marley "Sun is Shining"- This elevates my soul on so many levels

2. Frankie Knuckles & Jamie Principle 'Your Love' - something happens to my insides when I hear it

3. Marvin Gay "Whats going on " - So incredibly relevant for this time.

What are you most proud of yourself for and why?

My tenacity. I have a very very strong will and it has served me in times of absolute crisis. It has helped me get up every day and keep going. Being a single mum and business owner was a very complex system. Managing them equally was not always possible. Generally one or the other suffered at one time. I always knew when my daughter needed me most, and I would pull back on the focus of the business, and in times of business focus, I could give that more attention. The balancing act was one of the hardest things I've ever had to juggle. Financial strains were always a part of it, a fashion business is expensive to run, however I was lucky enough to be skilled in cooking and fine taste to make sure my daughter never missed out on the things that were important, like a very full belly, a beautiful home, wonderful friends and support network, lots of great music and dancing, and I think this truly is what i'm most proud of. My tenacity to keep going and make it all work somehow.

Christina Donaghue

Who is Christina? What are her origins and who would you best describe her as a woman of today?

I always find these questions so hard as 'I' feel like the sentient being, the spirit that sits behind Christina, the label given to the organic part—the shell. So I'll do my best to explain. I am a spirit who is having a human experience as a woman, a mother, an artist, a friend, daughter and lover to choose from. This lifetime I was born on the land of the Burramattagal at Parramatta hospital in 1977. My circumstances were complicated. My mother is the eldest of nine children in an Australian

Irish Catholic family whose people came to Australia as settlers and convicts from Ireland.

My mother met my father while travelling through Iran. He was an American helicopter pilot who had gone to Saudi Arabia and Iran to work for Bell Helicopter after the Vietnam War. So I am the descendant of African Slaves, the Cherokee and their masters (terminology allotted to the role they held). We have a remarkable history that traces back to the Appalachian Mountains in Tennessee and Virginia, Senegal and beyond. Our family dates to the first pieces of land farmed independently by freedmen, Hoop Creek. So, I am a Black mixed race person, illegitimate by legal status, who was born in the western suburbs of Sydney, and raised in a traditional Irish Catholic family. I grew up in Merrylands, Gilgandra and Cambewarra and from time to time Claxton Tennessee, USA.

I believe all this is relevant to speak about as it is foundational to the themes that have risen up in my life of connectedness to community, right to representation in the public sphere and the importance of identity in the development of the self. As a woman of today I am grounded. I know who I am and where I am from in terms of lineage and the expression of the universal whole. I understand the role of choice in how I choose to live each moment and that each choice will cause ripples that move outward, whether I see them or not. I live first as an individual as what is inside will equal what is outside and visa versa. I think I live next as a mother as my children are still very small and I am in a period of conscious parenting, helping them discover who they are and how to walk in this life in order to complete their journey.

I think I then live as a friend, lover, daughter and community member, endeavoring to engage mindfully and compassionately in those relationships in a way that is balanced and proactive. Within the system in which we live I recognise my enacting of each of these roles and choices is innately political and rebellious which becomes increasingly so when I write, create, speak and perform my 'being' on this land.

What is your profession? How did you end up in the industry you are in and what do you love about what you do?

I don't know if I have a profession per say, it's one of my problems with limitations—I suspect that is so for many people. I am an artist, a creator, I guess storytelling covers what I have always done. I've just finished a truckload of degrees around journalism, media and creative writing specialising in poetry and the African diaspora in Australia. I act, I dance, I write, I paint, I draw, I sing, I make music, I produce theatre, I take photos, I lead community organisations, I sit on NGO panels and speak for this community....I could go on. So, I condense all that into the title of multidisciplinary artist and community advocate. I ended up in the arts industry because I never wanted to do anything else. I don't think creativity or art is what you do so much as what you are. I started acting when I was in highschool, putting together drama teams, reading poetry and monologues in competitions and eisteddfods on the south coast of NSW where I lived. I did everything that you could do at school.

I'm a prolific reader. I'm a prolific writer of all forms. I did Rock Eisteddfod (Bomaderry Highschool, look it up). I was part of every school production. I did street theatre. We wrote plays and performed them for other schools. Then from age fourteen I started travelling to Sydney on the weekends to model. I moved to Sydney when I was about seventeen and just started going for auditions while I was working and studying. I got a talent agent and started going to countless auditions as a way of life, which is something I do to this day. I joined a girl group, started producing music and dancing. From there I ended up working as a professional Hip Hop dancer and singer for years. I am constantly engaged in self education. I did classes at ATYP (Rebel Wilson and a bunch of other now successful actors/singers were there at that time) and the Actors Centre.

I have always believed in being a lifelong learner, constantly working on my crafts because I just love it and the tribe that comes with it. It wasn't until after having children and them being in primary school that I completed formal education in writing, photography, sound, digital and journalism. What I love about what I do is that it is an expression of my soul, it's connected to my own life experience and it has real world impacts. It is in line with my own personal mission and contributes to the self healing of the living world. So, it uses my passions and channels them into the work of improving and protecting the world in which we live.

You are a woman of many talents and skills which is something that is so admired and inspirational to others. Your love for creative and raw talent has

seen you merge between the worlds of dancer and thespian with ease. Outside of your creative life you are also a mum to two beautiful girls and are a woman that is fearless, determined and passionate to live life on your terms. You have overcome many hardships and challenges to get to where you are today and continue to survive and thrive. How do you balance the challenges of womanhood and your own personal evolution to make life work for you?

Nothing is separate, it's all the same thing. Everything that I do should be an expression of who I am and I try to stay true to that. I have a very loud spirit or inner voice and I listen to it. I believe that everyone has an amazing inner compass, if you learn to listen to it and not let the voices around you drown it out you will stay in balance. In terms of parenting I am really clear on how it is not what we say to our children that makes the greatest impact, it is what we do. So, how I feel about myself is more influential than what I say. I have to know who I am. I have to support my growth. I have to look prioritise myself first in order to be able to give to others. I accept myself with my faults and virtues unconditionally. I am not cloudy on any of these points.

As women we are challenged in very particular ways often.

When I left my long term relationship due to domestic violence our safety and wellbeing became my number one priority. Then as a mother I went about creating the conditions for healing. I created stability in our lives and that meant moving away from my community and projects that I loved. I created a routine. I set up a support system for us. I educated myself on parenting, relationships and the psychology of abuse. At no time did I panic because there's time for everything under the sun, and prioritising needs is important for everyone. As Madeleine Albright said, "I do think that women can have it all, but not all at the same time." Going to university at age thirty-seven as a single mother of two was daunting. That same year I acted in three productions and was running the school P&C almost single handedly. It was crazy, but organisation was key as was doing one thing at a time. As the years have gone by I have become more effective in my organisation and learned how to distribute work evenly over time. And I multitask, I'm that mum that you see at swimming practice with a laptop on her knees writing essays or catching a nap in the car in the twenty-minutes before school gets out. I do what I have to do and I don't apologise for that.

Also, I am open with everyone about everything. I don't play it off like it's all under control. My house was messy, my kids hair was barely done, my blessed lecturers have given me SO many extensions over the years, but I'm extremely open about my life and pressures and people around me have bent over backwards to help me achieve my goals. My daughters have complained all the way, but I just keep focussed on prioritising myself and I am teaching them the same. I don't think I have habits and routines, but really I do. I'm great at creating space for myself to be introspective. Most mornings you can find me in the garden staring at the plants, insects and lizards and drinking coffee. It's my meditation. I touch the earth every morning. I am really aware that there is something larger that I am connected to and I take time to identify my needs in relation to that. I think mental/spiritual quiet is very important in relation to being able to hear yourself and the universe. Which connects to me knowing my needs to be able to prioritise them. In the years since I found ways to include my own loves and needs into our life. I started working with the local community theatre group to produce plays and musicals. When my girls were school age I went to university. Now we're back auditioning and they too get involved in creative projects. And we've built a really strong community where we are. I have done so many things that seemed impossible to others and sometimes to me.

When I set out on those journeys I quite often laugh and say I don't know how I'm going to do it, but I'll do it. What do you think are the most important characteristics when it comes to creating a life on your terms and at times going against the usual stereotypes of life? A knowing that there is not one way to live. The imagination to vision and create a life for oneself that does not refer to or constitute anyone else's happiness or approval than your own other than an incidental byproduct. A consciousness that infiltrates everything you do thereby making your decisions intentional and directional. The willingness to be uncomfortable and to suffer the disapproval of others, I remember developing the 'fuck it' attitude when I was twelve after becoming conscious that no matter what I do in life someone is always unhappy with me, so approval can't be a condition of living. But, I have also found that when you live with non-judgement, compassion and love, you show kindness and gratitude without discrimination I am often overwhelmed by the amount of people, circumstance and things that show up to help me create that life that I envision.

As a woman of creativity, passion, strength, ambition and determination, how would you best describe what success means to you and do you feel you have achieved success in your life?

Success to me is simple. Success for me is being present in this life that I'm creating in every present moment. I definitely can't come up with a definition that is attached to things, having sat with quite a couple of deaths now there are things that are very apparent. All you have is the relationships and the moments that you create. Peace, beauty, love, acceptance, connection, laughter and authenticity are all things that resonate with my definition of success. I have always loved Maya Angelou's definition, "Success is liking yourself, liking what you do and liking how you do it."

What are the 5 things you cannot live without?

Time, Love, Laughter, Food and Water.

The motto or mantra you live your life by?

Just trust. No matter what crazy things have gone on in my life, "just trust" is always that inner voice for me. And everything is always perfectly designed, even if I can't see it at that moment.

What advice would you give to the teenage version of yourself, 18 years old and just about to embark on your life's journey?

Stop buying clothes and cosmetics, buy property and make passive income. Write your own plays and produce them now. There is no how to, no one has any idea what they're doing, they're just faking it. Pick up a camera now, you love photography. Party on! Dance all night, you'll get in dodgy situations but you'll make good choices. Don't waste so much time on the back up plan, go and wholeheartedly do that thing that makes your soul sing. Your mother will never understand you, stop trying to make her. You'll never fit in, don't worry about it.

Three songs that speak to your soul?

- My Life - Mary J Blige I'm Here -
- The Color Purple Golden - Jill Scott

- Lovely Day - Bill Withers
- Lauryn Hill MTV Unplugged 2.0
- India Arie - Everything

(I know that's more than three...I could keep going)

What are you most proud of yourself for and why?

It sounds basic, but just for not giving up. Getting from one end of the day to the other seems like a massive achievement everytime I lay down to rest. And looking at all the days between the first and this, I'm very proud that I made it this far.

Melissa Dooley

Who is Melissa? What are her origins and who would you best describe her as a woman of today?

Melissa is a Mum. A daughter. A sister. A best friend to many. And a loyal partner to just one. I am of European/Irish background and a 2nd generation Australian on my Mum's side. I best describe myself as a very loyal, honest and compassionate person who greatly dislikes injustice. I will stand up for what I believe and struggle seeing people suffer unnecessarily. I have a soft spot for the elderly - even the grumpy ones

- and have an appreciation for being born into a free society and given the opportunities to grow into the person I am today.

What is your profession? How did you end up in the industry you work in and what do you love about what you do?

This is an interesting question for me, as I've had a few different professions, and my current one has played an extremely small part in my life, however somehow managed to have the most impact on me personally. My reason for getting into the industry is also my reason for wanting to leave. After being self employed and my own boss for 6 years, I decided to rejoin the workforce and secured a job as a strata manager for a small team in my local area through the recommendation of a person, at the time, I quite admired. That admiration sadly disappeared quickly after I witnessed and experienced the unprofessional way this person behaved in their role. And as a result, I lost a great deal of respect for the company (or more so the management of that company) for whom I work for. I began in the role with so much drive and potential to do well, but over time became worn down by the negativity created by the one person who was supposed to be supporting me. The negativity they put out around us made me feel like they got joy from seeing people fail and this affected my ability to perform.

Instead of building us up, they strived to tear us down. Their behaviour caused me to suffer with my development in the role and in turn I struggled to complete my job to the best of my abilities. So unfortunately I have very little that is positive to say about my time in this profession due to my introduction into that job and just grateful for some of the friendships I formed during my time there.

As a woman of passion, strength, loyalty and determination, how would you best describe what success means to you and do you feel you have achieved success in your life?

100%. Success to me is feeling complete and confident in the direction my life is heading and trying to stay positive even when things are getting me down. I'm a dreamer at heart and happily sail through life being content and grateful with what it has offered me. I am a "glass is half full" kind of person and strive to find the silver lining in everything. Success is what you choose it to be and I choose for it to be happy and positive. Happy that I am lucky enough to have very supportive and loving parents, amazing and incredible friends around me to lean on and laugh with, and the tools to navigate through life's challenges.

What are the 5 things you cannot live without and why?

My Mum - because who doesn't need their mum! Mine is one of THE best. She made me into the person I am today and a lot of my best attributes were learnt through watching her go through life. She is always there for me and I am truly grateful.

My Son - because he is the greatest gift on earth and he fills my heart.

My friends - because they fill me with joy and happiness. Spending time with my friends (especially on weekends away) rejuvenates my soul.

Love - because being in love and being loved is one of the greatest feelings in the world.

Travel - being able to explore the many wonders and cultures of the world and experience new and exciting adventures.

The motto or mantra you live your life by?

Live the life you love and love the life you live! You only get one go at it, so make it worth living for!

What advice would you give to the teenage version of yourself, 18 years old and just about to embark on your life's journey?

Enjoy every moment and don't let anyone try to dim your shine.

Three songs that speak to your soul?

This one is quite hard for me to answer. As my Mum liked to say to me "What song isn't your favourite song!" Lol. Music has such a powerful way of controlling your emotions and altering your moods. I love music that gives me those "feel good" moments. And I especially love music that gets the hips swaying and the feet moving, because I LOVE to dance.

A song that I really do love is "Broken Arrows" by Avicii - it has such an uplifting feeling. Also "Feel Again" by One Republic - again another very uplifting song. And "Let's Dance" by Chris Rea - because I just wanna dance :)

What are you most proud of yourself for and why?

My friendships. I am proud of the friendships I have formed over the years with some amazing individuals. Finding people you can count on to be there for you when you need them and being able to be there for people when they need you is something I value greatly and am lucky to have this in my life.

Mariam Freig

Who is Mariam? What are her origins and who would you best describe her as a woman of today?

I am an Egyptian woman born in Cairo, Egypt in the mid-80's, currently existing at a point where I have begun to embrace myself as I am and finally live in the feeling of confidence and joy whilst experimenting to understand my purpose.

What is your profession? How did you end up in the Entertainment Industry and what do you love about what you do?

I don't actually work in the entertainment industry despite it may seem that way, I am currently working in banking with a foundation in photography, I'm a creative soul deep down. My network of friends and contacts spill widely into the entertainment industry both here in Australia, Los Angeles and Dubai which has allowed me the opportunity to be involved in many pockets of the entertainment world, where my heart is.

You are a woman of many talents and skills which is something that is so admired and inspirational to others. At the core of everything you do, you have a great heart and fierce love for your family and your beautiful Egyptian culture. You eat life but have also overcome many challenges to get to where you are today. How do you best balance the art of personal evolution and being an entrepreneur to make life work for you?

Only now at 34 am I seeing that I have been living a nomad type of life which was a hard idea to reach as I am a person that thrives off stability as much as I simultaneously thrive off spontaneity and living in the moment.

Life for me is one big confusing contradiction, sitting on fences and seeing situations from both sides which has made clarity a hard thing to achieve. My "work life" has definitely taken a backseat to the personal turmoil I had allowed myself to live in, the entire 5 years so far that I've been living in LA, and my life in Sydney leading up to my move stateside in 2015.

In all honesty.. I can't answer this question so much as I haven't achieved that balance yet but I can say this; personal evolution is a real thing, a beautiful thing and an incredibly powerful journey to experience and it only happens when your mind and soul are open to a higher energy and a belief in trusting the universe, not believing in the phrase "bad timing" – some things may seem like bad timing (according to your plan) yet they are happening exactly the moment they are supposed to.

What do you think are the most important characteristics when it comes to creating a life on your terms and at times going against the usual stereotypes of life?

- Confidence – in yourself, in your beliefs and your way of doing life

- Tough skin – the ability to deflect discouraging behaviors and opinions of others

- Determination – tackling and getting past all the curveballs life will continuously throw at you, not letting it break you and moving forward on a steady foot

- Vision – to see what it is that you want and work backwards to achieve it

- Understanding – that not everybody will understand, not everything is for everyone

As a woman of creativity, passion, strength, ambition and determination, how would you best describe what success means to you and do you feel you have achieved success in your life?

Success to me is accomplishment in multiple facets of life including financial, physical and spiritual well-being. The financial ability to live life freely, on my own terms and to allow for my close tribe the ability to do the same. Success also means remembering the things that matter no matter how bizarre life gets - family, health, loyalty and unconditional love.

If you asked me a month ago if I feel like I have achieved success in my life my answer would have been no. You're asking me now, yes I do feel so – my family knows I love them despite my daily distance, distance as I am focusing on grounding myself, listening to myself and speaking on how I feel as I feel it as second nature now, whilst building my financial foundation with focus.

Finally, a tribe that will see you through life no matter the situation, no more the time of night you call to; vent, make no sense or debate something out. I've come to learn that a solid circle is everything and I'm beyond grateful for mine, over anything else.

These are people who make you feel like everything will be ok even when your world is burning down, have faith in you when you have none in yourself, embrace and love you the exact same as if no time has passed, even when if has been years in between.

What are the 5 things you cannot live without and why?

Music, Faith, love, human touch, money, mental freedom (food) – sorry I cant count, these are the main components that I feel make up my inner being.

The motto or mantra you live by?

Throw yourself into the feet of the future you, envision how you want your life to be and work backwards to create that.

Think smart, don't think with your heart.

Be fu*king kind.

What advice would you give to the teenage version of yourself, 18 years old and just about to embark on your life's journey?

Plenty! But to sum it up... be confident, you are greater than any thought you have of yourself. Be brave, be loud, don't feel like you are taking up space... own the spaces you enter and the ideas you have because you are rare, heavily loved and such an exceptional woman. The world needs somebody like you, as strong, powerful, different and level-headedly soft-hearted as you.

Three songs that speak to your soul?

- Speak – Jhene
- Redemption song – Bob Marley
- Whats going on – Marvin Gaye

The last choice could be heavily influenced by the current state of our world.

What are you most proud of yourself and why?

Diving into my own soul and learning myself, as opposed to catering to others first - Allowing myself to feel what I feel without masking it, releasing it in the moment and letting people who need to know, know how I feel – not letting situations linger, taking them in my stride and move on, after all... Shit happens, life always goes on baby.

Emprezz Golding

Who is Emprezz Golding? What are her origins and who would you best describe her as a woman of today?

Emprezz Golding is of Jamaican parents, who was born in Australia. I moved back to Jamaica at 2 years old and then returned back to Australia at the age of 12 via the USA, where I completed High School, College and my early musical /entertainment career. Then I moved to the United States where I worked as an international brand agent and then back to Jamaica to pursue my ultimate career, creative endeavours and social development goals.

What is your profession? How did you end up in the Entertainment and Youth Advocacy Industry and what do you love about what you do?

My current resume reads as follows:

- Corporate Social Responsibility Consultant
- Television Host & Executive Producer/ Director
- TVJ Host- Jamaica's #1 Morning Show, Smile Jamaica
- Board Chair; Maxfield Park Children's Home
- Board Director; Edna Manley College of the Visual and Performing Arts
- Board Director; NCB foundation
- Youth Advocate
- Entrepreneur
- Project Manager/Developer
- I make things happen
- Motivational Speaker

In regards to my achievements within the entertainment industry I have had Record Deals in Australia and came back to Jamaica and started working with a TV Cable

Station. I partook in live music performances and then went to the major network TVJ as the host of the Magnum Kings and Queens of Dancehall Show, which is where I then created the show and social enterprise, Talk Up Yout-Giving the Youth a voice. From there I began hosting Jamaica's leading morning Show 'Smile Jamaica', which then eventually led to my role as an in-demand speaker and host at major events across the island.

You are a woman of many talents and skills which is something that is so admired and inspirational to others. Your list of achievements and successes run long and varied as you continue your life's work dedicated to the youth of your country of Jamaica, ensuring they are raised to be strong, confident, empowered children growing up in safe communities. Using your platform as a TV anchor you have used your power of positivity to reach so many and help to educate and inspire so many in your community.

You are also a proud wife and mother of two beautiful children whom you are raising in the same light of self-pride and confidence. Your journey has been one filled with ups and downs and

in these challenges is where you have found your voice and your purpose to inspire. How would you say you are making the balance of motherhood, career advancement and your personal evolution work for you?

I don't believe in balance. I believe in Juggling and you have to Juggle well. When one ball is up the other is in the middle and one is about to hit the ground, you have to change direction and change the game regularly.

What do you think are the most important characteristics when it comes to creating a life on your terms and at times going against the usual stereotypes of life?

Make it a commitment to design the life you want and create your own life commandments and values. Be afraid of no-one.

- Live with Intent
- Live for a purpose
- Serve your country and your people
- Let no one distract you from your goals
- Reclaim the fallen

- Search for the truth that has not been shared openly.

The commandments I developed that I live by and share in my motivational speeches to all I connect with.

1. **Thou Shalt Build Partnerships**

2. **Thou Shalt Show Gratitude**

3. **Thou Shalt Execute**

4. **Thou Shalt Risk Failure-** Take a risk and be ok with the consequences of your failures. Consequences & failures are teachers & guides....

5. **Thou shalt be on time**-Don't waste time & Opportunity
   'Early is on time, on time is late, and late is unacceptable.'

6. **Thou Shalt Market yourself-**Your reputation is usually all you have sometimes

7. **Thou Shalt Think BIG** –what man has done man can do... Limitations are in our minds hold us back

8. **Thou shalt never stop learning:** No matter how old you are or how long you've been in business, you never stop learning.

9. **Thou Shalt Say Achoo-I am Allergic to negativity**

10. **Thou Shalt turn a profit**

As a woman of passion, strength, loyalty and determination,, how would you best describe what success means to you and do you feel you have achieved success in your life?

Success is living each day doing one thing towards your goal. I feel I am successful. If I help one person a day, I feel successful.

What are the 5 things you cannot live without and why?

1. A Present mind- This keeps me sane, Close to the creator, At one with nature, Mindfulness

2. A Vision and a Mission - without it, you are walking dead.

3. Food & Water- Keeps us nourished

4. Family- Companionship, Laughter, Stress relief

5. Friend who are like family- Companionship, Laughter, Stress relief

The motto or mantra you live your life by?

Live with JOY. (My Mother's name - I now live to honour her after losing her last year. She was inimitable)

What advice would you give to the teenage version of yourself, 18 years old and just about to embark on your life's journey?

Don't spend money on material things you see in marketing campaigns. Invest in land and other assets, that will turn a profit.

Three songs that speak to your soul?

1. You Bring me Joy
2. Mama Africa
3. Natural Woman-

10. What are you most proud of yourself for and why?

Proud to be alive and give and dream. This is life. Proud to make people smile and find their own joy and purpose in life.

Karen Griffin

Who is Karen? What are her origins and who would you best describe her as a woman of today?

Today I am proud to say that I am happy and comfortable with who I am. I have probably been the harshest critic of myself over the years both personally and professionally and have learnt many lessons good and bad along the way. I'm not afraid to speak my mind or my truth whilst being open to listening to different points of views and opinions. I think I am a good listener and a mediator, always trying to find a positive solution or outcome to a situation. I'm determined and hard-working. Once I start something, I can't leave it half done!

I try to live my life with honesty, integrity and kindness. I am passionate about many things including my fiancé, family and friends as well as the love of my horse Jimmy, 2 dogs Kobi & Brontye and my cat Charlie and of course my business that I have built and run for over 17 years now.

What is your profession? How did you end up in the Entertainment / Media industry and what do you love about what you do?

I am originally from the UK and my parents are Australian and English. I spent the first 20 years of my life in England where I went to school and later studied media at college before moving to Australia in 1995. I had been working for a boutique record company called Scratch Records since 1991 after I left college and decided I wanted to travel to Australia before settling down into my career. I spent 6 months in Australia before I started working for the Hilton Hotel and later the Sheraton on the Park where I ran promotions for their nightclubs. It was at Riva Nightclub that I reignited my love for live music and the entertainment industry and commenced working with independent tour promoters as well as the Star Casino where we launched Cave Nightclub and ran various club nights.

In 2000 I decided it was time for a change, I had been approached by a producer / songwriter (Andrew Klippel) who was setting up a new record label with James Packer called Engine Room Music and decided this was the challenge I needed, I missed working in the record company environment and saw this as a positive step forward. I worked with Engine Room for nearly 4 years, as a small company I had various roles and whilst I loved the diversity, I missed feeling that sense of achievement you have when you are accountable for something specific.For years people had always told me I should get into PR, I was a good 'people person', was organized, attentive and patient but to be honest back then I had no idea what PR even was! I was offered a contract role at the PR agency that had represented the record label, I was really there as a filler until they found a 'qualified' publicist to fill the role or so I thought....

Six months later and I knew this was exactly what I was meant to be doing. I loved the challenge and enjoyed working with the media, I still get that sense of excitement when you know you have placed a story and you see it come to fruition. I enjoyed my time at the agency and the experience it gave me, I just wanted to combine what I had discovered to be my dream job with the experience I had in the music industry.So, in 2003 in my late 20's with little fear back then and a lot of ambition IDENTITY PR was launched, and I have never looked back.

You are a woman of many talents and skills which is something that is so admired and inspirational to others. You have been a respected PR director of your own company Identity PR for many years, have worked and represented some great talents within the entertainment world and also navigated your business through some incredible highs and lows to always come out the other side as a consistent and trust brand. How have you managed to balance the art of entrepreneurship and your own personal evolution on a woman?

There have been many challenges along the way, a lot of anxiety and stress to keep the business afloat. At times not knowing where your next pay-check was coming from or how I was going to pay the staff. In the beginning, I knew nothing about running a business and trusted the contractors and agencies I hired to guide me, that didn't always happen and a few years ago I found myself in a big financial hole. I sort the help of a new accountant who has literally saved me and my company. He didn't sugar coat anything, he saw where the mistakes had been made and he also made me solely accountable for the decisions I had made and how things has transpired in the company, it was a hard lesson but one of the most valuable I have had and together we have come out the other side and 17 years on I am still operating and have an incredible list of clients to my name that I have absolutely loved working with.

The original purpose of the agency was to help support artists and brands that I admired and was passionate about in the media. I loved being part of a bigger team but being accountable for one aspect of it. Working with international superstars was exciting but so was seeing an unknown artist break through and build a profile because of the input you had as their publicist.

What do you think are the most important characteristics when it comes to creating a life on your terms and at times going against the usual stereotypes of life?

For many years the business was the priority, I threw myself into it, travelled between here and the U.S to work with clients in both territories and fell into the trap of being married to the job. People always see the glamorous side of PR, the events, the celebrities, the red carpets but don't see the hours and hours of work that go on behind the scenes, the media never stops and neither do we so it wasn't always easy to find a balance.

I have luckily always found my escape and (sanity!) when I am with my animals, going for long rides with my horse or just being around him and generally spending time at the stables has kept me grounded and helped me recharge the batteries. Being near the beach and walking Kobi would help clear my head but it probably has only been in the last 4 years since meeting my now fiancé that I really value this time to disconnect from work and enjoy a balanced life. We travel a lot (pre Covid-19!) to discover new places either in Australia or overseas and it really helps me to stay focused when I'm back at work. I'm a lot more 'present' when I'm with family and friends now too.

You have to be really disciplined on both counts to not get so caught up in work that you lose focus at home and vice versa. Time management is imperative and ensuring you take time for yourself, if it's a morning walk to start your day or meditation (I have never been good at settling my mind and get easily distracted so for me a beach walk is more suited). Everyone is different and everyone operates differently, I try not to compare myself or judge myself / business against others and focus on what I do and can do for my clients, that has to be the priority. I am a big advocate of supporting others (especially women in this industry) and working together opposed to being competitive.

As a woman of passion, strength, loyalty and compassion, how would you best describe what success means to you and do you feel you have achieved success in your life?

Success to me is doing something that you love, it may not be easy and will challenge you but if you really enjoy what you do and strive to do the best that you can then you are on the right path. As long as I'm still growing, learning and feel passionate about the clients I represent or the personal goals I set myself then I think I'm doing ok.

What are the 5 things you cannot live without and why?

- Music – It has been there every step of the way and tells my life story.

- Laughter – Can get you through most situations if you can find the humor

- The Beach – The sound of the ocean has always been my 'go to' place when I need to clear my head.

- Love – The love of my husband, family, friends and fur kids are everything to me.

- Hope – we all need this, especially now when our world feels like complete madness

The motto or mantra you live your life by?

Appreciate what I have, express gratitude and know that nothing good comes easy. You can have anything you want if you put your mind to it.

What advice would you give to the teenage version of yourself, 18 years old and just about to embark on your life's journey?

- Don't take things personally.
- What others think of you is none of your business!
- Don't be afraid to try and give something a go
- Be proud of who you are
- Trust your instinct every time, it won't let you down.

Three songs that speak to your soul?

This is so tough!!

- Prince and Purple Rain - An all-time favourite artist that I have loved from the beginning and have had the privilege of seeing live on several occasions, this is definitely up there for me.
- Marvin Gaye – What's Going On – There are so many great tracks from this artist but especially at this time of turmoil his lyrics to this particular song speak volumes.
- INXS – Never Tear Us Apart – Simple and haunting and a personal favourite.

What are you most proud of yourself for and why?

I am most proud of myself for not giving up, even at the toughest of times with the business and when my anxiety was literally going through the roof, I had to find a way to get through. I didn't have anyone to fall back on, it was me and it was literally sink or swim.

A few years ago, I worked with Kevin Liles the former President of Def Jam Records and co-founder of 300 Entertainment, he has an incredible attitude to life and business that is truly inspiring, his motto 'Make It Happen' is what I try to keep in mind whenever doubt creeps in. It would have been easier to walk away, get a job working for someone else and not have the additional stress and worry but that wasn't why I started the business, I wanted to make a difference and I hope I have done that.

Dora Gutierrez

Who is Dora? What are her origins and who would you best describe her as a woman of today?

I am a woman – Mother, Sister, Daughter, Friend, and Business Owner. I come from a large extended bi-racial Colombian family. My immediate family (mum, dad, and siblings) moved to Australia when I was just 2 years old. I describe myself as a woman of today as I am raising my son on my own, I am mum, dad, housewife, and breadwinner in my home. This is the norm for many women today – fortunately, as women, we are in a position now where we are creating our own opportunities and we are strong enough and supported enough to do so.

What is your profession? How did you end up in the Fitness Industry and what do you love about what you do?

I'm an Entrepreneur, Group Fitness Instructor, and Personal Trainer. I never imagined that I would end up being in, working in let alone running a business in the fitness industry. To be perfectly honest, it all started shortly after my son was born – I was not in a good place. My sister suggested I try working out; I was a new mum who was absolutely lost, I was sad, alone and I had no direction - I'll admit that at first, I didn't enjoy it – but once I realised that working out was more about the psychology everything changed for me. I started to love it and thrive off it. My sister asked me to help her with a project she was working on at the time and before we knew it, SaltoFIT was born; my second baby. Seeing the physical, emotional, mental and positive changes SaltoFIT has had on people in particular women is the most rewarding part about working in the fitness industry; I can see myself in every single woman that embarks on a brand-new fitness journey with us and it is rewarding beyond measure

You are a woman of many talents and skills which is something that is so admired and inspirational to others. At the core of everything you do, you have a great heart and love your family to the inth degree. You are a mother to your gorgeous son and have overcome many challenges to get to where you are today. How do you best balance motherhood and entrepreneurship with your Saltofit brand to make life work for you?

Thank you - For me, motherhood and entrepreneurship are very similar; they both require a great deal of time, effort, and unconditional love. They require late nights and early starts, giving up late-night drinks with friends and constant reassurance that "you're doing a great job" – to be honest, it's hard to find a perfect balance but being present for both is at the heart of it all. My son who is 5 knows all about my business, the logo, the songs, the locations, and even the members – it's been very important for me that he sees the hard work and love that I put into my business, I also think it's important for him to see first-hand what it takes to look after your health, your family and your dreams.

Teaching him as I learn has been a great way to devote time to him and the business.

What do you think are the most important characteristics when it comes to creating a life on your terms and at times going against the usual stereotypes of life?

I've only recently come to realise that I need to "back myself" when making decisions in life and business. There have been many times in my "working" life where I have thought to make a suggestion or stopped myself from saying something aloud as I didn't think what I had to say was good enough or that anyone would see any value in what I had to say – only to have someone else make the same suggestion and it is successful or action something I had already thought of. Other times when I did speak up I was talked out of my "gut" instinct only to realise I should have stuck to it. We, as women are always taught to listen and be "ladylike" not to make too much noise or cause any waves, I am now recognising that I need to back myself, make those waves, that I need to be confident in what I think, and that my gut instinct is a genuine tool to help me get ahead in life. This for me is probably the most important characteristic. Cliché, as it may sound, believing in yourself, is invaluable. If you can't believe in yourself, no one else will – not your kids, not clients, not your competition, and certainly not any potential investors.

As a woman of creativity, passion, strength, ambition and determination, how would you best describe what success means to you and do you feel you have achieved success in your life?

A successful life to me is living a life you are proud of. One where you have balance and freedom. I don't believe that I have achieved full success yet – but I know that I am on the right path. Success to some means lots of Zeros in their bank account, but I've met a lot of people who have that and are unfulfilled and unhappy. I have achieved success in becoming my own person and loving the path that I am on. Having those zeros in my bank account is definitely a bonus but by no means a true measure of my success.

What are the 5 things you cannot live without and why?

1. Kisses and cuddles from my little boy
2. Daily SaltoFIT session (I'm not just saying this! It's true!)

3. Cup of tea

4. My phone (unfortunately)

5. Super-hot showers

The motto or mantra you live your life by?

"You become what you think about most of the time."

What advice would you give to the teenage version of yourself, 18 years old and just about to embark on your life's journey?

Study more, party less, and travel often. Lay foundations and SAVE some money! Don't rely on a man to sweep you off your feet – sweep yourself off your feet!

Three songs that speak to your soul?

- Video - India Arie
- Superwoman - Alicia Keys
- Hush - Goapele

What are you most proud of yourself for and why?

I'm proud of myself for picking myself up from a moment and situation in time that I thought I would never recover from – I felt debilitated and I couldn't see myself coming out the other end. Not only did I recover from it, but I ended up discovering myself and realizing my true potential. I'm proud of myself for raising a kind and caring young boy with nothing but love in his heart. I'm proud of all the women I have helped through my business SaltoFIT and I'm proud that even having gone through everything I've been through I still hold so much love in my heart.

Tracy Hinckson

Who is Tracy? What are her origins and who would you best describe her as a woman of today?

Well, I was born in Georgetown Guyana which is located on the continent of South America. Half of my ancestry comes from the beautiful island of Grenada, part of the Caribbean. Although we are on the continent, we are considered West Indians because of our close ties to the Caribbean through a history of slavery and the British empire.

I would describe myself as a proud black Guyanese/Australian woman, socially conscious, spiritually connected, daughter and most important a mother. I enjoy life even when faced with adversities, coming for a strong line of black queen's so I always know I always draw on their strength when needed.

What is your profession? How did you end up in the industry you work in and what do you love about what you do?

I work for the NSW government doing administration work, how I ended up in this industry was by chance of applying for the job. I enjoy the work we do, we are a place where people can come to hold medical providers accountable for the care provided. With saying that my job can be quite stressful as you deal with complainants' raw emotions when discussing experience with a medical provider.

You are a woman of many talents and skills which is something that is so admired and inspirational to others. You are also a fierce, opinionated, passionate and determined woman who says what she thinks and stands up for what is right. You are a mother to an amazing young man, but also a mother whose journey has been fraught with many

things that has not always made your journey easy. Through it all you are an independent warrior woman who has always done what is right for your son and your relationship. How hard has the balance of motherhood and self been for you?

Thanks, my sister I feel like I have lived 20 lives from the death of my mother at 19 to losing my son. These experiences have shaped my life as losing my mom at 19 when a young woman needs that guidance into adulthood was hard. Not having a good family support base was here in Australia made that journey at times very difficult. I have always believed that the truth will set you free, and also narrate your own story so others cannot create their own version about you. Being a single parent to a child with ADHD/ODD has been a struggle with daily incidents with school and home, I almost lost my son to the system due to the lack of support for kids with this diagnosis or their families.

Trying to get a work/life balance with a child with ADHD is very difficult as you are always in a heightened state because you always worry about what people will say about you and your child when he misbehaves. It has taken a toll on my social life as I limit my time with folks because of his diagnosis. It is the hardest thing to see your child struggle to have long term friendships and not be able to read social que when interacting with his peers and adults.

Being a person of colour it really was an eye opener how the court system operates with people of colour and cultural sensitivities and the we know better attitude really was an eye opener for me as a woman, mother with a child where the system tried to separate me and my child forever. I had to lean on my ancestors and faith to get me through these tough times, I was determined I was not going to be broken and I was going to show these people they don't know me. I come with generations of strong women who have walked through fire for their kids.

What do you think are the most important characteristics when it comes to creating a life on your terms and at times going against the usual stereotypes of life?

I think the most important characteristics are being happy, being truthful with yourself and those around you. I don't do fake friendship and as I have gotten older I find now I really enjoy being different I was never a follower so if that goes against the stereotypes I am cool with that analogy

How would you best describe what success means to you and do you feel you have achieved success in your life?

Success to me means being able to be comfortable with self (i.e. your life choices, family, relationships). I have been a work in progress aiming to achieve my life success but always keeping my faith and integrity in the forefront

What are the 5 things you cannot live without and why?

My son, my god, my music, my friends and myself.

My son is the greatest achievement he has completed a void in my life and made me whole. Faith is something I celebrate privately with prayer, silent meditation and the positive words. My music helps me to express my feelings whether it's Hip Hop, R&B, dancehall, calypso, jazz it lifts or soothes my spirit in times of trouble. I am blessed with the friends I have in my life, they have supported me and cheered for me when I needed a squad.Believing in me supporting myself through thick and thin has given me such belief that I can survive anything that comes my way in life.

The motto or mantra you live your life by?

Stay black, stay strong but most of all enjoy life.

What advice would you give to the teenage version of yourself, 18 years old and just about to embark on your life's journey?

Wow, I lost my mother at 18, I was lost and scared of everything but masked it with irrelevant things and people. I think I would have told her to know your "Value and Self-worth", heal your soul, live your life and enjoy life's experiences. Most important advice would be "YOU will survive" all of this pain you are feeling right now and keep going no matter what happens in your life you are her daughter and she was a warrior as you will become.

Three songs that speak to your soul?

- Step back, let god do it – Dr Charles G Hayes & The Cosmopolitan Church of Prayer
- My Life – Mary J Blige
- Black beauty – Beres Hammond

What are you most proud of yourself for and why?

Being a mother, gosh when I think about my life without my baby boy it's not the same. He was the best surprise in my life. Although my journey has had many ups and downs I believe god doesn't give you more than he thinks you can handle.

Zaidee Jackson

Who is Zaidee Jackson? What are her origins and who would you best describe her as a woman of today?

I am a strong willed South African born woman that has been raised by two incredible parents. I was raised to strive for my greatest desires through hard work, tenacity, integrity and faith. My personality is strong. I'm unapologetically passionate about my family and friends, my career and my personal projects. I am a believer in treating people how you would like to be treated. People that know me would say that I am an honest straight shooter who sets boundaries to ensure that respect is paramount. My goal each day is to show up for myself. To wear my badge of honour each day ensuring I'm walking a path of purpose. Showing compassion and heart whilst displaying an honest representation of who I am as a woman.

I'm a fierce believer in being accountable for actions and stepping up to the plate in owning everything I do. I am known for holding people accountable should they treat me with disrespect, something I simply will not tolerate.

I was taught to own my space, stand with courage, respectfully and, with intent, live a life I can be proud of. Being comfortable in my own skin, in my own company is part of who I am and I celebrate it. It really is about me trusting myself, owning my gut feelings and the belief I have in myself.

What is your profession and how did you start your journey in the paper and printing industry?

I was on a mini sabbatical from working in Sydney to be in Melbourne when my eldest niece was to be born. As the universe would have it she graced us with her presence five hours after I arrived from my long road trip. That day I felt a love of another kind for the first time for this perfect little girl.

Three weeks later I realised I actually needed to start working and applied for a job at a paper company. The plan was to simply work whilst in Melbourne for a few months and head back to Sydney. Twenty-four years later I continue to enjoy, stay challenged, gain rewarding experiences in a position of sales and marketing role. As a mentor and educator in an ever evolving industry of paper and print I have found opportunity to give back to an industry that has afforded me so much.

My role as a Business Development Manager is to work within the Design community, engaging, influencing, creating inspirational experiences relative to paper and print.

Our team enjoy working with the creatives throughout Australia on a myriad of incredible projects, bringing them to life through out technical experience and creative input.

We work with some of Australia's largest brands, and have the privilege to work with some of the world's most talented designers.

Part of my role is as a keynote speaker at industry events representing our company and elevating our position in the market. Sharing knowledge with the community on our products and business is a terrific experience. I produce the events for the business along with my team and enjoy the feeling of creating market activations.

I thoroughly enjoy my role as an industry lecturer within the university and tafe institutions working with students studying for a Bachelor of Design degree and Design Diploma.

Working with the students and creating opportunities as a mentor is one of my more rewarding contributions in my career. Something I am extremely proud of.

You are a woman of many talents and skills which is something that is so admired and inspirational to others. Out of all of your creative talent, be it candle creator, poet and celebrant, how does Zaidee Jackson survive and thrive through them all?

My love to express my creative side is what drives and fulfils me. Writing poetry enriches my soul. It allows me freedom of thought and emotion. There's a book waiting to be written but there is time for that.

I find utter peace in losing myself when creating scents and producing candles that enhance people's homes. What started off as a hobby for relaxation, coupled with my marketing knowledge, I'm redefining my brand and excited to relaunch it to market. I placed it on pause when my grandmother "Mama" passed away a few years back. We used to spend such a beautiful time together, working to produce my first range of candles.

A way to move forward and honour her, I decided to make some changes to the brand and am looking forward to re-launching.

Becoming a Civil Marriage Celebrant really has enriched my life. I'm a romantic at heart, I love sharing the moment when two souls connect in front of their community. I believe in love. It is an honour contributing to life celebrations and special milestones in people's lives.

My practice in meditation, mindfulness and some structured diary scheduling keeps my balance. I know my own limits and ensure I create sacred moments for myself. These are the times I cherish. Reflection time in my life is when I find peace and clarity. My creativity is heightened through a process that works for me. Meditation for me is key.

What do you think are the most important characteristics when it comes to creating a life on

your terms and at times going against the usual stereotypes of life?

Being unapologetic with who you are and knowing your strengths for me is part of the course. Each day for me is about keeping with the sentiment of being open to learning something new. Staying humble but honest with yourself and striving to always put your best heel forward is a vibe I choose to step to.

Having an amazing support crew in my family that keeps me grounded and that I know loves me unconditionally makes my focus remain sharp. I have an incredible close group of friends that I go to for council. With both my family and friends I am not afraid to ask for help. It's part of surrendering to a higher good and knowing you simply don't know all the answers.

Also, not walking a path with fear as a limitation rather as a companion to drive me through those moments when I pause, assess, reflect and act. When my stomach steps into a curve I literally pause, breathe, assess and use that feeling as fuel.

Being kind, calm and staying in my lane, respecting others and knowing who I am is part of the journey. I don't allow others to determine how I feel about who I am. Quite frankly I have been taught that others' opinion of me is none of my business. So I forge the path of Zaidee Jackson with broad shoulders and a heck of a smile!

As a woman of passion, strength, ambition and loyalty, how would you best describe what success means to you and do you feel you have achieved success in your life?

Thank-you for this question and I appreciate you acknowledging attributes in me as a person that I am proud of. Success to me is shaped in many forms. It's having a happy and balanced family life. It's been able to experience life with my family on our terms. To dictate how we shape our journey. Whether it be a personal or professional experience, it is the way I have engaged with and achieved outcomes that enriches both.

It's been able to plan a life fully accepting that there are pivots along the way. Knowing how to adapt in a moment is a successful journey for my mental health. I have always been complimented on my strength and courage to undertake directions in my life. For me, I create a pathway of purpose and in that alone comes my success. Anyone can attain financial reward and attribute it to success but for me it's the long play.

If I have created a legacy for my nieces and nephew and ten God children to follow their heart and always strive to soar to be their truest version of themselves, then my life thus far has been a successful adventure.

What are the 5 things you cannot live without and why?

- My family is my world. I believe you choose your parents and I struck gold when I was born into my family. They are the colour in my day when darkness comes and they are the reason I want to create happiness in our world.

- My faith as a Christian. This has been a steadfast part of my life. I have been raised in a family that prays together and supports each other as a priority in life.

- Meditation practice in the morning and evening keeps me balanced and focused in the life I have created for myself. It's one of my favourite times of the day.

- Music keeps my soul at ease and feeds my creativity. The lyrics in songs and how they tell the story allows me to get lost and escape sometimes.
- Writing is my most personal expression of articulating my thoughts and emotions.

The motto or mantra you live your life by?

Know your worth, define you on your terms and always come from love in all you do - Zaidee Jackson.

There are others that I keep on me at all times here are two I subscribe to deeply.

"We are what we think. All that we are arises with our thoughts. With our thoughts, we make the world."- Buddha

"It takes courage to grow up and become who you really are." E.E. Cummings

What advice would you give to the teenage version of yourself, 18 years old and just about to embark on your life's journey?

No matter the circumstance or situation to be unapologetically authentic in every way. Never allow fear to be your limitations rather the reason you step outside your comfort zone to continually challenge yourself. Surrender to the universe and trust yourself like no one else can. Back yourself and never let others' opinion of you define your outcome.

Carve your pathway, never give up on dreams and always know you are supported by your close knit circle. If you fail at something, say thank-you for the lesson, assess the learnings and apply it to the next attempt.

Don't settle in love for the sake of it and never underestimate your worth as a woman. When you get in your feelings, own it, feel it and then sashay the shit out of a fabulous pair of heels.

Your worth is defined by you alone and your mirror reflection is the most wondrous thing to be proud of.

Three songs that speak to your soul?

The following songs take me to places for different reasons. They all have a purpose to get my vibe right and allow me to feel present.

1. Blessed - Jill Scott
2. I am Light - India Ari

3. Just Fine - Mary J. Blige

What are you most proud of yourself for and why?

My fierce appreciation for my family and the support we provide each other. We make each other a priority. Always staying true to myself. Even as a younger woman I knew what I wanted and had an innate ability to feel when people or things were not in my life authentically. I did and still do understand the value of myself and my worth. When the exchange in a relationship is no longer of equal value, I know when to walk away. Never out of anger or feeling hurt, from simply out of respect for myself

My career I have worked hard to become successful. Today I still have a passion for what I do and am blessed to work alongside some incredible people. I'm proud of my ability to lead and develop individuals to become the best versions of themselves.

Mostly I'm proud of my unapologetic way of owning who I am and what I stand for. Heels and all!

Maya Jupiter

Who is Maya? What are her origins and how would you best describe her as a woman of today?

My Father is Mexican and my Mother is Turkish. I was born in Mexico and migrated to Australia when I was one year old. I have family in Turkey, Mexico, Japan and the US and my immediate family is in Sydney.

I grew up in a working class, multilingual household where I was taught the principles of the Bahá'í Faith. The oneness of mankind, equality between all races, women and men.

I was twelve years old when my parents put me on a plane to Tokyo to visit my Aunty and her family. All of this has informed the person I am today.

I am opinionated, independent, loving, passionate, empathetic and always open to learn.

I see things holistically, and understand the intersectionality of struggles. I fight for social justice to make this world a more equitable and safe place.

What is your profession? How did you end up in the Entertainment Industry and what do you love about what you do?

I am a Hip Hop Artist, a TV and radio presenter, and co-founder of Artivist Entertainment.

I always knew I wanted to work within the Entertainment Industry. I took a Music Industry course at TAFE when I was 19 to learn as much as I could but my path was forged through life experiences. I love making music that is used as a tool for change, I love the energy of live performance, I love supporting and uplifting artists that don't get mainstream exposure but have something really important to say.

You are a woman of many talents and skills which is something that is so admired and inspirational to others. As a proud woman in HipHop you have held court in both your communities in Australia and LA as a spirited artist of truth, conviction and above all else authenticity of self through all you create. You have inspired so many in your journey, never letting up on creating and sharing your HipHop message through the narrative of empowerment. You are also a wife and mother to two beautiful children and have to monitor their digital footprint in a social media frenzied world whilst also sharing parts of your life with fans, friends and family on an even keel. How has the balance between motherhood, artistry and your own personal evolution been for you?

This is the big question! It is so hard to find balance, I think it's a constant struggle and it changes as you go through different stages.

When I became a Mother, I was still trying to finish an album. I remember giving myself 3 hours on a Friday to work on it. That's all I could muster in the first couple of years. My husband travels a lot for work so I am the primary caregiver of our children. And I wanted to be. I wanted to take a year to settle into the role of Mothering but I was also warned of "not losing yourself."

I actually think this is not helpful advice. I'm never going to lose myself because I know exactly who I am. However I do agree that if you don't do things for yourself every now and then, as a woman, you can become depressed and feel unfulfilled. For me, it looked like taking time (when I was ready) to join women's groups, go on a retreat and focus on healing and inner growth. It all takes time, and it's a constant search for the right balance. Mum guilt is so real.

In terms of sharing on social media, I don't really share about my husband or children. So it does feel inauthentic at times. Instagram gets a very curated, one dimensional part of me, the Artivist. It's hard as I want to protect the privacy of my family, yet I do have a desire to be my whole authentic self online. I'm still figuring out the right balance.

What do you think are the most important characteristics when it comes to creating a life on your terms and at times going against the usual stereotypes of life?

You have to know who you are, what you want, and what your values are. Sometimes this means imagining new paradigms.

In the early 2000's commercial radio told my label that "Australians weren't ready to hear an Aussie accent rapping." We all know this to be false. I knew the talent that existed in the underground hip hop scene and I knew of many Indigenous and non-anglo artists who had a lot to say but weren't given the platforms. I made it my mission to get their voices heard on tv and radio.

At this present time we are being asked to reimagine entire structures of our society and to reflect on our own privileges and relationships. We can all make huge shifts in our culture, but it will require courage, determination and persistence.

As a woman of passion, strength, loyalty and determination,, how would you best describe what success means to you and do you feel you have achieved success in your life?

Success is being happy, healthy, being able to contribute to my community in a positive way and make a positive difference.

Success is raising outstanding human beings who will continue the fight for social justice and will lead with love.

Yes, I do feel that I've achieved success, I do what I love while being of service to my community.

What are the 5 things you cannot live without and why?

1. A good cup of tea. It's so grounding and can become a ritual for quiet alone time. Also great with friends.

2. Dance - I am a dancer first before anything else. Moving my body is medicine and an everyday practice.

3. Music - How else can we process our emotions and feelings?! I can't live without listening to it, singing along to it, writing it or performing it.

4. The Beach - there's something about the waves, being in the water, listening to the sound of the waves crashing, tasting the salt, and being immersed in the ocean that makes me feel at home.

5. A great story - Whether I'm reading, listening to an audio book, podcast or watching a tv show. I love losing myself in someone else's story.

The motto or mantra you live your life by?

I know it's cliche but; *"Be the change that you wish to see in the world."* - Mahatma Gandhi and "Love is the Answer" - Aloe Blacc

What advice would you give to the teenage version of yourself, 18 years old and just about to embark on your life's journey?

You are good enough.

It's ok to say no, boundaries are healthy.

You can't save everyone, so stop that shit.

Love yourself.

Three songs that speak to your soul?

- Ty - Somewhere, Somehow, Someway
- Briggs, Dewayne Everttsmith & Gurrumul - The Children Came Back
- D'Angelo - Africa

What are you most proud of yourself for and why?

I'm most proud of doing the work to heal myself. I'm still on my journey, but it takes a lot of guts to look in the mirror and reflect. I want to heal myself and the lineage of women who came before me. I carry their stories in my body and I want to make it a little bit easier for my children and the generations to come.

K-Sera

Who is K-Sera? What are her origins and who would you best describe her as a woman of today?

K-sera is of Scottish / Lithuanian descent so I like to think of myself as an Outlander/Viking warrior. I began my career as a dancer then MC in a crew called Bad Rep many years ago. Simultaneously entering a career in radio and realizing I was never going to set the world on fire as an MC but could play my part in promoting Hip Hop in this country by infiltrating radio nearly 20 years ago. So I basically swapped mics.

What is your profession? How did you end up in the Entertainment Industry and what do you love about what you do?

I am now producing 6 x shows a week for The Edge in Sydney as part of Australian Radio network I host 4 x shows live weeknights on the Edge and K-sera & The Dirty Dozen is still the only Hip Hop show on a commercial radio station in the country. I manage 18 DJ's The Edge Mix Masters. I am assistant Music Director for The Edge and Program Director of iHeart Old Skool which is actually one of my favourite stations. Basically over 5000 of my favorite old skool tracks check it out if you get a chance.

You are a woman of many talents and skills which is something that is so admired and inspirational to others. As a proud woman in HipHop you have held court in the radio game for two decades, dedicating your life and passion to bringing stellar music and news to the HipHop community in Australia. You have helped and inspired so many in your journey, and even though your own journey has been one filled with adversity and challenge, you have continued to push through barriers and fight for what is right in every arena of life. How

has the balance between your own journey and a woman in HipHop in Australia and that of your personal evolution been for you?

I guess as a woman in Hip Hop for so many years my journey has been one of overcoming bullies and haters and those clout chasers that I think we all have at some point in our lives. There have been many highs and lows. I am now no longer the people pleaser I used to be. I have learnt to set boundaries and cut ties with those who were toxic to my growth. I am also a very private person and that's why any social media I share is about the show and the artists not photos of me or my private life. I think familiarity breeds contempt and what I do is about the show and the artists adhering to the philosophy that "Hip Hop should educate on a higher level and promote positive change through music." So what I am wearing or eating is not really relevant!

What do you think are the most important characteristics when it comes to creating a life on your terms and at times going against the usual stereotypes of life?

I am not really like anyone I know so I guess I have just inadvertently created my own path and have always been the exception to every stereotype and I guess I say as much when I sign off every night with "I don't stop never quit". Also my pride is strong and I am never one to not hold my own.

As a woman of passion, strength, loyalty and determination, how would you best describe what success means to you and do you feel you have achieved success in your life?

My success is based on always fronting up and getting the job done and still being able to do what I love is success enough. I don't have it all but I definitely have enough and constantly remember to vocalise my gratitudes for all that I have in this life.

What are the 5 things you cannot live without and why?

Music, friends, family, phone & weed (legalize it ffs)

The motto or mantra you live your life by?

I have 2 mantra's;

"Live in the moment and embrace change" & "It's not what you can say yes to but what you can say no to that will separate you from the rest."

What advice would you give to the teenage version of yourself, 18 years old and just about to embark on your life's journey?

Don't date boys you meet in the yard, if they cheat on you or beat you, leave their ass asap, and focus on what you want not what everyone around you wants.

Three songs that speak to your soul?

How does one just limit it to 3 songs lol! There are so many but let's start with 3 albums;

1. Brother Ali- undisputed truth – Puzzle or Pedigree are 2 of my favs

2. Beatnick & K-Salaam The World is Ours – favourite track Papoose ft Busy Signal – We gotta take it or Talib Kweli – Feel

3. Eric Sermon – Chilltown New York – any track is dope

What are you most proud of yourself for and why?

I am proud of myself for literally staying alive and still keeping it moving and not killing anybody in the process.

Missy Kay

Who is Missy? What are her origins and who would you best describe her as a woman of today?

Missy Kay is vibrant, bubbly, peaceful and yet powerful all in one. Born in South Africa – and although I was raised in Australia, my parents raised us as if we were still back home. So, I refer to myself as a proud South African Australian. I am a woman who dances to my own beat … usually there are many in my head lol but lately I have been actively listening to the compliments I receive, and I am learning that my presence is uplifting, nurturing and mesmerising. To me I am just authentic to myself and loving the flow that comes with.

What is your profession? How did you end up in the Music industry and what do you love about what you do?

I found myself having to sidestep from my business and get back into the corporate world due to how the lock out laws heavily affected the entertainment industry which drastically plummeted my operations of my DJ Agency – Funk Ink by 45% in the first year and 80% in the second year. At the moment I am exploring the corporate world as I study Leadership and Management with goals already set in place to relaunch another business model once I graduate next year. I have also already started one podcast and planning on launching another shortly.

Although my original reason to start Funk Ink was to continue on my brother's legacy, I quickly found my purpose being directed to remove the exploitation of Art and put the power back into artists' hands ensuring that DJs would be able to have secure careers and retire with a pension. This was my driving force that created a deep passion to achieve such a vision, but I ultimately love what I do because I love the form of turntablism and DJing. It is something I was always drawn to and at one stage learnt the basic skills but was just naturally drawn to the business side of things because I am great at multitasking and coordinating details.

Here is a silly story ... I was bullied so much in high school that instead of allowing myself to continue to be sad and lonely at lunch breaks I went to the administration office and asked if I could help with anything, so every lunch break I just went and worked in the office. I was heavily influenced by my mother's creativity and father and brother's entrepreneurial successes.

You are a woman of many talents and skills which is something that is so admired and inspirational to others. You have held various roles in your journey thus far, from being an event promoter to radio show host and beyond. Everything you have done has always been from a platform of the utmost respect for the industry and people you work with and of course your love and loyalty to upholding your late brother's legacy is something that never

goes unnoticed. You are honest in the moments of challenge and adversity you go through and share with your platform your journey with a transparent narrative that always looks at the glass half full. You love your family and friends fiercely and always stand up for the truth, even through your own pain. How has the balance between womanhood and your own personal evolution been like for you?

WOW, reading your perspective of me just made me sigh in relief. Like a release of pain. I believe you captured this question with your comment of "through your own pain" … I think the balance has finally been found through the freedom of breaking each and every glass ceiling I have let anyone create above me due to others realising my own potential before I did and being threatened by that potential. I learnt only recently that I have been naïve in believing the best in people not realising that it's easier to bring someone down than encourage someone to achieve greater.

I have always been authentic … passionate, vulnerable, open and direct from a young age and it took me what feels like forever to have realised that people do not like that because it makes them have to self-reflect and not everyone is willing to do that ... It was learning to be comfortable in my strengths instead of someone else's discomfort that has brought me the balance that I truly needed. I cannot deny that I am an empath that feels emotions as though my heart is actually bleeding ... so I am grateful that through all the struggles along the way I have had the presence of strong and fierce women to learn from and seek guidance from.

I will never forget when my business was picking up but I started to lose "friends" I became very ill. I reached out to Mirrah Reflects, someone whom I have admired from such a young age. I wrote her a long ass Facebook message telling her she doesn't know me –I needed her and wow did she come through!! She showed up for me in so many ways and I was just merely a stranger to her.

What do you think are the most important characteristics when it comes to creating a life on your terms and at times going against the usual stereotypes of life?

Bravery is definitely one ... but the thing with me is I never saw myself as brave, courage or confident yet these are three words people frequently use to describe me I think the biggest thing is knowing yourself, understanding who you are, your values and what you stand for or will not stand for is what will help you achieve greatness in your life.

Being able to self-reflect, being transparent with yourself and taking ownership to change takes a lot of courage too. So being willing to keep yourself accountable to yourself and in the trajectory of your goals will also help with creating a life on your terms. I also truly believe that being raised with the family values has made me resilient. Growing up this was tough because I am such a sensitive soul, however as I make my way in this

world of business, I have found it to make me agile and fluid with changes around me. I have become a woman who can think quickly on my feet and is extremely resourceful. Mix that all in with creativity and as an entrepreneur you will find yourself kicking goals and setting a higher bar of standard for you and your employees.

As a woman of passion, strength, loyalty and determination, how would you best describe what success means to you and do you feel you have achieved success in your life?

Success is always evolving to me and I learnt that when my business downsized. I felt so lost and I felt like such a failure, but I checked in with myself. I reflected and kept a journal for a year celebrating each day to remind myself that success comes in so many different forms and levels and it's ultimately all about timing really.

So yes, I have achieved success, success that a lot of people do not actually know about. From rock bottom trying to figure out where I was going to get my next cheque to make rent to now living in a place I envisioned, designed and built for life. I share amazing moments with my parents, something that I took for granted but when I compare that to my brother's passing and my sister living overseas, I cannot help but see that rebuilding my relationship with my parents as great success.

What are the 5 things you cannot live without and why?

1. My family – because when you lose a family member nothing else can replace that endless hole like family who share a similar burden, plus none can love you and yet call you out for your craziness quite like family! =)

2. Nature – because the beauty of her presence is magical and keeps me dreaming eternally.

3. Peace of mind – because without internal peace I would not be able to who I am to so many people.

4. Ambition – because I am a natural born leader and without it, I would have no essence to life.

5. My friends – because life would not be the same without laughter, fun, silliness and adventure! And although you can do these things on your own ... it's just not the same. Being able to laugh and cry with someone you can trust and grow with is indescribable and possess a level of value to one's soul that I pray daily everyone in this world gets to experience.

The motto or mantra you live your life by?

Together we can make a difference is my business mission statement but lately what's been getting me through life has been "Your vibe attracts your tribe" ... so whatever is meant for you in that moment of time will be and nothing is wrong with separation ... reason, seasons, lifetime blessings – let them keep rolling!

What advice would you give to the teenage version of yourself, 18 years old and just about to embark on your life's journey?

Don't change or stop for nothing or no one – if it doesn't feel right ... don't wait around until it does – just keep on pushing forward until you get comfortable within yourself and for yourself! You do not need to overextend yourself to make people see you, remember to put your own oxygen mask on before you help others because at the end of the day – ain't nobody going to save you but your momma and only you can help yourself back up!

Three songs that speak to your soul?

Hahahahahahahha – I am the worst person to ask this question to because I have too many LOL .... But here goes:

- Janet Jackson – Together again
- SWV – Right here
- Shola Ama – Still believe

What are you most proud of yourself for and why?

Never giving up on myself even when I lost hope ... because griping up to sharp edges helped me to continue to develop personally which has shaped me into profoundly high-spirited woman. It's helped open me to experiencing the magic around us which is limitless and simply electric.

Gladys Kibone

Who is Gladys Kibone aka Kween G? What are her origins and who would you best describe her as a woman of today?

I pay my respects to the sovereign people of this land and the Gadigal people and I honor the elders' past, present and future. The daughter of Godfrey Namokoyi & Alice Nabusayi of the Bugisu tribe from eastern Uganda. I was born on the land of my ancestors who I honor everyday. Gladys if you already know me but I introduce myself as Kween G Kibone I am The Sensible Rebel. I have always wanted to be doing everything I am doing today even living by my alias is bringing into existence what I envision.

I am a fierce warrioress bought here to disrupt the status quo and bring love and light and raise the voices of the marginalised and decriminalized the innocently criminalised!

I have been living this Hip-Hop lifestyle and remained passionate and deep rooted in persisting to exist beyond the status quo. I am an artist wearing my different hats. My first love is the microphone I rhyme and write songs and perform them in many forms and lately it's been through live music. I started the year in a band where I was invited to join by Sengelese drum & dancer Yacou. The band AfroMbollo had a residency in January 2020 at LazyBones Lounge on a Thursday night and it was so incredible to move beyond my usual capacity to share this African musical excellence, we had the place dancing. I really get to use my skills as an MC through freestyle but also reprogramming my music and singing in the Waloff language of Senegal.

Today I am finding that I have grounded myself to be living a lifestyle that has moved me through this journey of life. I am happy to say that I am surrounded by so many sisters black sisters who value the same thing, living in love for humanity.

What is your profession and how did you start your journey in the Entertainment Industry?

Profession- Performer/Producer/Facilitator/Curator. I started my journey on the radio. That's where I realized the power of the microphone and the ability to deliver music and word to whoever is listening. I learnt how the industry worked through networking and saw that as a gateway to get out there with my own music and also the people I knew who had music to play. My intention has always been to break through the barriers and hold space for melanated & marginalised voices and stories.

It was the music I was playing that politicised me to think critically about the world we are in. Dead Prez album Let's Get Free began my journey to decolonisation.

I perform my original music mostly produced by ZDE longtime friend & collaborator. When I'm on a live show it's with dancers Double Trouble- Geny and Lady Chicka, two sisters who have leveled up the Sydney dance scene and I have recently started performing with an all female band. When I am not on the mic I am a trainer in radio passing on the skills to people interested in producing their own shows. I ended up doing that through many years in community radio as a presenter/producer and other roles. I started when I was 16 and learned the ropes eventually landing a national radio stint producing music and current affairs programs.

I love making media and after 2year hiatus I decided to use the pandemic to produce a podcast titled Postponed Not Silenced. This was a response to a canceled march that I was set to MC on March 21st for The International Day for the elimination of Racism and Discrimination aka Harmony Day. Australia may be only the country that doesn't call it what it is and I am a part of the Inner West Multicultural Network and we decided we say there is No Harmony in Racism and that was the beginning of the podcast and now I am 5 episodes in. Postponed Not SIlenced covers how the response to the pandemic has racially discriminated against people in our community and the most recent episode speaks to the real pandemic, Racism. It is also a learning resource for people who want more. Postponed Not Silenced received the 2020 NSW Premier's multicultural Communications Award

One of the most exciting moments of the last two years was joining the Red Rattler Theatre as their bookings coordinator and it has allowed me be a put on some amazing shows with International and local performers and one of those is Dancey Dance Time which started with 20 people who danced till the end of the night to now over 200 people attending. Dancey Dance time brings culture and POC and QPOC world class dancers to present their original works with no restrictions! Dancey Dance Time is a team with Le Prime Apparel & GK Entertainment.

I am passionate about women's representation in music particularly in hip hop and by inviting WOC performers and collaborating to put on shows like International Women's Day at LazyBones 2020, Artivista Feb 2019, Candy Royalles Holla-Back 90s Throwback party. I currently sit on the advisory panel for the Australian Women In Music Awards.

You are a woman of many talents and skills which is something that is so admired and inspirational to others. You are also a mother of two beautiful children and an activist when it comes to human rights, indigenous affairs and a proud African woman who supports her people in the arenas of events, promotion and the arts. What are your thoughts on how you survive and thrive balancing

both your motherhood journey and your career that has seen you help others for many years now?

I grew up watching my father being a part of African Communities Council (ACC) going to meetings and organising the sydney African community, he was also an adult educator teaching computer skills. I have always been a part of communities in some way and that's where I have seen the need for visibility and raising and sustaining cultural awareness through arts. That's where it comes from for me and my father raised us and still gave his time to the community and that is something I have adopted. Trust and Acceptance the key to accepting what is given to you and trusting in what you do.

I'm a mother artist and it's just like any other career you go to work, you take care of the family and all that has to fit in, it's just done differently because our hours are not necessarily 9-5. The most empowering part of raising my children is being their first teacher and in exchange I am a learner because raising them has exposed me to many things and made what I thought was unbelievable to be believable. That you can still be yourself and love others. Balancing this with spirituality has supported me through the challenges that arise and looking to be the person my ancestors are calling me to be. In all this I don't take credit for all that I do and I have been and informally mentored by other women and people in various roles from media, music and not-for-profits that have given me the guidance and courage to go forward.

What do you think are the most important characteristics when it comes to creating a life on your terms and at times going against the usual stereotypes of life?

Knowledge of self! Having principles and values and understanding what those values are. Making sure there are elders and mentors in your reach. When I started my journey to decolonise and unlearn I discovered that a lot of what seems to be reality is not for all. Discovering that I can belong in a space where I once couldn't has encouraged me to want to spread the word that we must continue to stand against injustice and carry on the messages of the free thinkers and freedom fighters. The status quo wont live no more!

As a woman of creativity, passion, strength, ambition and determination, how would you best describe what success means to you and do you feel you have achieved success in your life?

I think the way success is defined is not ideal and I don't live to succeed because I have learnt that the model to success is not a fair path for all. I have stayed committed to this journey and found many people along the way who are doing so much work in our communities and witnessing that is a high achievement dedicating one's existence to be selfless and give time & energy that's achievement. Yes I believe that I am ready to achieve and still to achieve much more.

What are the 5 things you cannot live without and why?

1. My children - we are attached for eternity
2. My ancestry My Family- If I don't know who I am things will confuse me
3. My gift to write stories and improvise- This gives me energy and is a means of therapy
4. L.O.V.E- Levitate Only Vital Excellence
5. Environment/Climate/Mother Earth- I believe we are all here to take care of her

The motto or mantra you live your life by?

We are the makers of our own destiny!

What advice would you give to the teenage version of yourself, 18 years old and just about to embark on your life's journey?

Ohh yeah I often have this yarn with her and I say don't walk away when it's too hard, stick with it you will get better at it. Stay solid and stick with your family because you may drift too far away one day and you will find yourselves with nothing to say to each other and may forget what makes you most happy.

Three songs that speak to your soul?

- Jah 9 - The greatest threat to the Status Quo
- Dead Prez - I'm an African
- Barkaa - Our Lives Matter

What are you most proud of yourself for and why?

Winning the IQ2 Debate "Is Capitalism Destroying Us" with Alan Swartz, we beat the guy who coined the term "virtue signaling'. As I mentioned hip-hop politicised me and the opportunity to kick knowledge in a topic that is a beast to society and is the cause of economic imbalance.

Eva Links

Who is Eva? What are her origins and who would you best describe her as a woman of today?

Eva is a woman born in Australia to Lebanese migrant parents. She is the fourth of 5 children with never a dull moment growing up. She is now married to an amazing man and a very very proud aunt of 10 nephews and nieces, 1 grand-niece and 2 more grand-babies added to our extended family so I am beyond excited.

Whilst raised amongst a culturally insular community, My parents were thankfully welcoming and encompassing of people of all races. This definitely contributed to the formation of a diverse multicultural extended family, where the corners of the world are represented.

I have been with my current employment for 26 years and am still passionate about my work. I strive for the highest outcomes for youth and will not settle for sloppy or lazy work.

I have around 10 women in my life whom I will refer to as my "best friend". I am wealthy in love and support and am surrounded by some of the fiercest women around.

Amidst nieces, nephews, god children and friends' children, I try to lead by example of being a woman of integrity and upholding my value system, whilst at the same time striving to live a life with no regrets.

What is your profession? How did you end up in the Youth and Justice arm of the legal industry? (How did you end up working in this industry?)

I work with disadvantaged and troubled youth involved in the criminal justice system.

When I was fresh out of University after graduating, in 1991, I pursued work with young people. I was unsuccessful for over 30 job applications in this field and whilst frustrating at the time, I totally accept now that I had not yet been mature enough or emotionally prepared for the roles I was to embark on. After working in retail for approximately 3 years with continued unsuccessful applications to jobs in youth work, I quit my retail job to focus solely on chasing my vocational aspiration. I applied for what was referred to as "the dole" and went to the local CES and applied for the only job going in this industry. Some months later, I began my career working with young people in juvenile detention. As this work requires a lot of advocacy for young people, this was the start of my growth from shy, quiet, somewhat naïve girl to outspoken, forthright and expressive woman.

You are a woman of many talents and skills which is something that is so admired and inspirational to others. At the heart of everything you do, you have a great heart and are always caring for your beautiful god-children and your family and friends, always making sure people feel supported and loved. Working in such an emotional provocative job as yours and dealing with many challenges that come with your role, how do you best juggle the emotions that come with your job and also balance the various nuances in your life?

Switching off work is not always easy because I am human after all and I deal with real life stories, sometimes life or death, and above all, I deal with children,so my heart strings do get tugged very regularly. But I have come to accept that having this emotional response is not a bad thing as it means I have the empathy and compassion needed to do my job at its fullest.

I hope never to become unemotional in my job because should this ever happen, it means I have become desensitized and it would be time for me to leave. It would be grossly unfair to my clients and their families if I didn't have an emotional investment in their story.

Whilst dealing with youth who have sad stories, my focus with them is building their resilience, being solution focused, exploring their goals and helping them problem solve. It is a very rewarding job and we use a lot of humour with our youth.

Thankfully, I have mostly been able to have a good work-life balance due to having a very supportive, understanding and caring husband and family and friends that know when I am feeling good or not. Life gets tough sometimes, people I love get sick, relationships strain, I miss opportunities, I make mistakes but I am blessed enough to have many people in my life who carry me through all these, even when they don't realise they are doing it.

What do you think are the most important characteristics when it comes to creating a life on your terms and at times going against the usual stereotypes of life?

Do you! Or as Shakespeare once wrote "Unto thine own self be true".

Growing up, there were many religious, gender specific and cultural expectations of what a good Lebanese girl should be like. I went to uni where I made friends with women and men; I was heavy in the club scene; I had a wide range of friends most of whom were not Lebanese - all of these elements railed against what my culture expected. That wasn't a framework that I bought into wholeheartedly.

I trusted the path I was on even though it was different to that of my family and it would serve me well. I always believe that if you are yourself, you can not go wrong. It's too much effort to pretend to be someone you are not. And you will always be found out.

As a woman of creativity, passion, strength, ambition and determination, how would you best describe what success means to you and do you feel you have achieved success in your life?

The definition of success for me as I grow seems to broaden. In my younger years, success meant having a highly respected job (teacher, doctor, lawyer), buying a home, marrying well, having well raised children. For me now, success is bettering yourself no matter how big or small, any step forward is success. Not only that, but realisation and reaching a time in your life where you can be truly honest with yourself and self reflect is success.

What are the five things you cannot live without and why?

- My music – who doesn't love music. Slightly an obsession on my part, I can listen to rnb, soul and hip-hop 24/7. As I'm getting older, I find I am gaining an appreciation for a wider taste of music, especially Aussie Rock! (go figure)

- My books – fiction of course. It is not unusual for me to have up to 4 books by my bedside table. My reading time is every morning when I wake, every night before I sleep and any spare minute I get in the day. I have taken to listening to audiobooks in my later years when I drive or walk – just too many great books to get through.

- My high heels – the day I can no longer wear my heels is the day I will accept I have aged. Until then, I will walk like I am a 20 something strutting my stuff. And my golden rule, never ever take off your shoes at a bar, club, party no matter how much pain your feet are in.

- Potatoes – in any form - baked, fried, chips, mash, I will break any diet if potatoes are put in front of me. No will power whatsoever.

- Bush walking & Hikes – At a time when overseas or interstate travel is not an option, I adopted the attitude that I wanted to be a tourist in my own city. I joined a walking group and have been on some of the most amazing hikes through Sydney, the Blue Mountains, Tasmania, The Northern Territory and New Zealand. My hikes have extended to camping weekends and a whole new bunch of like minded friends with a common purpose. Now my mission is to convince my hubby to join me on these walks.

The motto or mantra you live your life by?

I'm a massive procrastinator and I often find ways to distract myself so I don't do a task I feel unmotivated for. A work colleague indicated this to be her favourite mantra and now it is mine:

"Just do it and it is done".

Not rocket science, so simple but so true. Since I have adopted this, my to do list has way more ticks in both work and life. This has especially been true for some of the uncomfortable discussions I have had to have with people that needed to be had.

What advice would you give the teenage version of yourself, 18 years old and just about to embark on life's journey?

At 18, you are not supposed to know how to do "life", so it is OK to fumble through it.

Life happens to you and you need to go for the ride. You need to take note and learn what things have made you feel great about yourself and keep building on those, and what made you feel low or horrible or uncomfortable and learn to stop putting yourself in those situations. It doesn't matter if you make the same mistake a few times, just keep learning and growing from it.

Three songs that speak to your soul?

This question was hard because I love love love music and there are many songs that get you right in the heart. But my three ultimates are:

1. Luther Vandross - So Amazing

This was and always will be my bridal waltz choice because it is perfect in describing how I feel in my marriage and in my relationship with my husband. Life has been so much more fulfilling and settled, less confusing since meeting my Prince. Plus, Luther

Vandross' voice is like velvet, he can sing "Mary Had a Little Lamb" and I will be moved.

2. Maxwell – This Woman's Work

This song is mesmerising, whoever sings it. But for me, Maxwell's version is exceptionally so because his voice is so soulful and pure. My understanding is this song was written about a woman and her baby in danger in childbirth and is sung in the viewpoint of the partner who is hoping they will make it through and regretting things he may have left unsaid. To me, this song speaks to the various hardships women can face and just how strong we are, but also knowing that the men in our lives love and appreciate us and we are important to them.

3. Michael Jackson – Off The Wall

Hands down my favourite Michael Jackson song and my favourite song to dance to. I don't care what is going on or who is talking to me when that song comes on, I don't care if I'm in a club, in a shopping centre, at work or walking on the street, I will be dancing like nobody's watching. I believe that song was written for me and my addiction to dancing until the lights come on in the club.

What are you most proud of yourself for and why?

What I am probably most proud of is the life I have built for myself to date.

Decisions that I have made and choices I have been confronted with have all brought me to this stage in my life where I have a lovely home, close family relationships, strongly formed friendships and a very rewarding and fulfilling career.

I have managed to establish myself in a balanced, happy, fun filled life. I take credit as this is achieved through my personal growth and self worth and not settling for less.

Mirrah

Who is Mirrah? What are her origins and who would you best describe her as a woman of today?

The best way to describe me is; I am a caring individual (wears heart on my sleeve) but not a pushover. I was brought up in a mixed family to respect and appreciate my Indonesian born origin with African American heritage. I was encouraged by my adopted parents and positive peers to practice daily mindful meditation & physical exercise to upkeep a healthy mind body & soul. Outdoor sports and dance were my favourite as a child throughout my teenage and young adult years. Meditation has assisted me throughout my years, especially now as a Black woman during our challenging times at present due to so many Black lives we have unnecessarily lost. May they rest in power.

What is your profession and how did you start your journey in the Entertainment Industry?

My self taught and inspired profession; as a creative artist through music, intertwines Blues; Soul, HipHop and twists of 80's Pop. Music was led from passion and was an active means for me to share stories through lyrics. Starting this journey as a youth, gave me a perfect escape with poetic expression to empower from my feelings. The word *'creative'* was unknown to me. I was just a passionate young person, who had found a way to process my thoughts through dance and written expression. I loved how it felt it had no boundaries. Then a professional path was introduced to me at 16 years old to tour with Public Enemy 1989 Fear of The Black Planet in Sydney; Australia with a HipHop Rapper as a backup dancer. That opportunity introduced me to the greats; Chuck D & Flavor Flav where I saw the power of word play and performance. Having them to grow into personal peers to share my performance skill was a positive thing to train further in how I can protect and serve HipHop the best way I saw fit. At 19 years old I moved to London; England and was ready to learn to be a part of the Entertainment industry. Not only as dancer, Choreographer and then an Emcee but as a young creative who was ready to be respected as an artist, writer and performer. 20 plus years later to present.I am proud of my personal accomplishments and excited to continue to learn, mature and blossom with each musical/ theatrical/written and vocal experience that continues to come to learn and accomplish financially to support my goals.

You are a woman of many talents and skills which is something that is so admired and inspirational to others. Apart from your artistry you are also a Youth Worker who is always engaging in the development of expression and self awareness when it comes to working with the Youth in your community. What are your thoughts on how you survive and thrive balancing both your artistic journey and that of shaping the youth of our future?

To survive and thrive with balance in my own artistic journey has had paths of prosperous opportunities and learning curves that has given me growth. There is no difference as an Artist, as it's bigger than HipHop and to be a Youthworker is just being a passionate Human. I have the same passion and responsibility in my life, music and youth work profession. I basically put in equal passion. Expanding on my meaning; my artist brand name is my birth name, mirrah (lowercased) describing my humble and continued student attitude and self reflection of self ownership.

As a HipHop artist, I practice my studies such as writing, reading, rehearsing, investing in vocal and singing training, researching history and being able to converse with HipHop pioneers listening to their HipHop history and culture, to then having this become apart of my mind body soul fully as my lifestyle. Investing in my Music, HipHop culture is as important and passionate as when I went to TAFE learning how to work as a Youthworker. It's bigger than the title. You learn responsibility and respect to empower and support young people from Indigenous cultures, and all young people around Australia with varied Faiths, upbringings and behaviours. To also learn how to be a part of a team with like minded carers, Youth workers and creative minds to support our future humans to aspire to their personal goals and to know they have safe people to inquire to, so their personal lifestyle can be a beneficial one. The most important balance to survive and thrive is our mental health. That is a practice and a respectful conversation to share to all ages to shape a healthy future.

What do you think are the most important characteristics when it comes to creating a life on your terms and at times going against the usual stereotypes of life?

The most important characteristics to learn from our youth to teen to adult is being your own ideal human. I feel *'authenticity'* is a great trait, to learn to experience and have ownership of who we really are is truly a life learning experience. Also acknowledging there is always space to grow & rebuild from mistakes. It's ok to not know everything. Adding *'humility'* to the list, you can be great and weak and that is a positive thing as it allows you to continue to practice and learn. It's so important to me to be Polite(manners are huge to me) being Considerate, Encouraging, Fair, Respectful, Responsible, Compassionate, Optimistic, Thorough and Courageous.

To have positive influencers to guide one and all to possess these traits naturally can make a better world to be positively loyal to all. These each may take time and practice. Most important is will. Especially when individuals may have not had that upbringing nor respected experience to know how to. This then is when we need the behaviours patience and personal perseverance to be able to actively spread this positive vibe and create a healthy environment.

As a woman of creativity, passion, strength, ambition and determination, how would you best describe what success means to you and do you feel you have achieved success in your life?

Success means to me for my individual growth: I aim to Solely Unfold with Confident Choices. to Excel, Sustain and feel Satisfied from my hard work ethics.

What are the 5 things you cannot live without and why?

5 things I couldn't live without:

- Healthy cared for Earth and Air
- Appreciative people with
- Authentic Positive mind states

- MUSIC &
- Delicious food to cook

The motto or mantra you live your life by?

My personal mantra: I am the creator of my reality; The core of my being aims to learn optimistically and value mine and others existence so we may live intentionally and forever evolve to vibrate a positive powerful vibration

What advice would you give to the teenage version of yourself, 18 years old and just about to embark on your life's journey?

Advice to younger self in a poem:

"Younger self, it doesn't matter, if school isn't you;

Stop disbelieving, keep reading, ask questions, Don't, fail you; Stay away from them drugs and dem fake friends;

Be aware of your wits, trust your instinct and don't doubt;

Live to the fullest and don't think life should end;

You're not worthless, you're full of purpose, have passion, and you're such a great friend; Shorti, like

HipHop, don't won't stop, be like a dope beat that captures and blends;

May you live intentionally forever to evolve and may your drive never end" -mirrah

Three songs that speak to your soul?

- SOHO; Hot music: sends the best dance vibration through me

- Judy Garland; Somewhere Over The Rainbow: Always has me tear as it makes me think of my birth mother (she's somewhere over a rainbow) metaphor to the unknown beauty that can lie ahead of all of our curious minds

- Dr. Martin Luther King Junior; I have a Dream speech

What are you most proud of yourself for and why?

I am most proud of learning how to survive my Anxiety. It has taken me years to acknowledge and prepare with patience, over standing and healthily overcome with mindfulness meditation, changing to a healthier plant based food routine and being honest to myself when I am not feeling at my best. Knowing I reflect a positive person for myself, is a great self accomplishment. Also realising to stop impressing others and just be an active positive person authentically. It really is easier to practice to be better day by day and have fun doing it.

Kristelle Morin

Who is Kristelle? What are her origins and who would you best describe her as a woman of today?

This is a tough one - I'm not quite sure how to answer this one haha

What is your profession? How did you end up in the Entertainment industry and what do you love about what you do?

I am a DJ, I have always been a music lover since I was young playing lots of instruments however I never really followed through with them until I started DJing. I've always loved the nightlife too. When I was of age I was in the clubs every weekend watching dj's how they moved the crowds and took them on a journey. It was at that stage then I decided I wanted to be a DJ... 20 years later I am still here. I love being a DJ as I love to see people feel the same way I feel about a track or a vibe. Watching the crowd groove to the songs I am putting together always brings me so much joy.

You are a woman of many talents and skills which is something that is so admired and inspirational to others. As a respected DJ, you have held your own in the genres of Afro House and UK House for many years, spinning in clubs and festivals around the world. You are a proud Mauritian woman who calls Australia home and is undeniably committed to building your legacy as one of Sydney's most loved female DJ's. Can you explain how the journey has been for you as you have learned to balance the art of entrepreneurship and your own personal evolution as a woman?

The journey so far has been fun, as with everything it has its ups and down. Starting DJing almost 20 years ago when there weren't too many female DJ's in the circuit was challenging. However it never stopped me from doing what I love most, if anything it pushed me to work harder. The balance is not something that has been difficult for me as music has always been a passion for me. I'd say the most difficult part of the journey was coming back to Australia - as the scene is still relatively small and having to almost build that again.

What do you think are the most important characteristics when it comes to creating a life on your terms and at times going against the usual stereotypes of life?

Be humble, be nice and be you. Don't try to copy anyone, be true to your craft, that's what makes us so unique that each and everyone of us can bring something different.

As a woman of passion, strength, loyalty and compassion, how would you best describe what success means to you and do you feel you have achieved success in your life?

Success for me is living my dream, and I can honestly say that I have done that. I remember when I started Djing my dream was to play in the cities where the music i played and loved came from, playing amongst my peers and mentors as well as travelling around the world to do that. Not many can say they have or are living their dreams... I can honestly say I have and this to me is success

What are the 5 things you cannot live without and why?

1. Family & Friends - I wouldn't be where I am now without them, my mom has been so supportive of my dreams

2. Music - it never lets you down, whatever I'm going through I know that it is always there gets me through the good times and the bad times

3. Travel - there is so much to be learnt around the world.

4. My Sneakers - I have an addiction, I can admit it.

5. Gratitude - there is so much for us to be grateful for.

The motto or mantra you live your life by?

Just do you and everything happens for a reason

What advice would you give to the teenage version of yourself, 18 years old and just about to embark on your life' journey?

Ahhh I guess be confident, follow your dreams and never settle for less than your worth.

Three songs that speak to your soul?

How can you ask a DJ this question?? I have so many songs that speak to me in each genre it's so hard to just choose 3 but here goes for 5 haha

- Love Can Damage Your Health - Telepopmusick (Dennis Ferrer Remix)
- Stay - The Controllers (Extended Club Mix)
- Crazy Love - MJ Cole
- Before I Let Go - Frank Beverly, Maze
- Circles - Zepherin Saint ft Nathan Adams

What are you most proud of yourself for and why?

I'm proud of myself for following my dreams, I left my family and friends and network and new country all to pursue my dreams. When I started DJing I told myself to play at the Annual Jamboree in Prospect Park,

Brooklyn. This is one of NYC's most respected House Festivals for over 20 years. I'll never forget when I finished my set I started crying from sheer joy of accomplishing that.

Tabitha Ojeah

Who is Tabitha? What are her origins and who would you best describe her as a woman of today?

My name is Tabitha Unekwu Sim Ojeah. My background is Nigerian. I was born and raised in Australia. I am a complex, free-spirited, creative young woman, a child of God aiming to live a life full of love as honestly and authentically as possible .

What is your profession? How did you end up in the Entertainment Industry and what do you love about what you do?

I'm a Recording Artist, artist named Tabi Gazele – I sing, write and record music. I was born into a musical family so I was exposed to playing and performing at a really young age, it's normal to me. In my late teens I started taking it a lot more seriously, after years of singing in church I started doing gigs and writing my own songs. I was receiving positive feedback so I decided that I wanted to do it for a living. I ended up studying music and then I've basically been learning and adapting rapidly while on the job ever since. I love that music has the power to connect in the most incredible way, it can make you feel things you've never felt before, it can bring back memories instantly, it can uplift your spirit. I see myself as a vessel to convey messages through music and I feel honoured to carry that gift.

You are a woman of many talents and skills which is something that is so admired and inspirational to others. Your artistry is honest, thought provoking and passionate and highlights the very essence of the woman you are. Your music and authenticity as an artist representing strong and empowered women of colour is inspiring and so needed in today's current climate and also lends to the narrative that your own journey has had its own

winding road of challenge and adversity to get to where you are in your creative freedom today. How would you say you are making the balance between artistry and your own personal evolution work for you?

Thankyou for that lovely acknowledgement. There has definitely been a windy road of challenge and adversity. I think now more than ever I'm really open to using the experiences of my personal evolution to fuel my artistry and inspire it rather than let it become a kind of hindrance and stumbling block. I used to chase perfection at all costs and I think that hurt me in a way because I found it really difficult to express myself and just let out anything and everything. The good, bad and painful stuff. Now I can draw on it to create new material

What do you think are the most important characteristics when it comes to creating a life on your terms and at times going against the usual stereotypes of life?

1. Know who you are, what you do and don't stand for first.

2. Keep your eyes on the goal purpose always and don't stop if the path towards it doesn't go as planned

3. Learn how to set healthy boundaries and be able to express those unapologetically

4. And basically, develop high Emotional Intelligence, never stop learning, trust your intuition, learn how to build a team and delegate the weakest parts of you, you'll be way happier and effective in the long run, have a grateful attitude, be kind, laugh a lot.

As a woman of passion, strength, loyalty and determination,, how would you best describe what success means to you and do you feel you have achieved success in your life?

- Success to me is discovering my purpose in life, why I get up everyday and being able to live my life according to it and being able to earn a living from it. I believe I have achieved a level of success already because for someone like me I've had to devote so much time and energy into discovering my purpose.... I thought for a long time it was just about becoming a well known singer but I've learned that I'm created for way more than that so I feel like I'm on the right path and that makes me happy. I just need to work on the financial side a bit more but I have faith that it's going to grow.

What are the 5 things you cannot live without and why?

- The Holy Trinity – I've tried living life on my own terms and I can't say I'm better off without it
- Phone – It's my connection to everyone, music and basically everything, I like to chat on the phone quite a lot.
- Moisturiser – I have dry skin.
- Hugs – I discovered I can't live without hugs especially in lockdown being away from all my friends and family. I had to buy a really cuddly teddy bear for these desperate times.
- Nature – As long as I'm around some nature to clear my head and breathe some fresh air, I'm good. I'm Australian, I love open air.

The motto or mantra you live your life by?

It's possible, just take one step at a time.

What advice would you give to the teenage version of yourself, 18 years old and just about to embark on your life's journey?

I would tell myself to listen to God first and always, let him order your steps. Don't try to please everyone and grow up too fast, take your time to be present in each moment. Find out who you really are and what truly lights up your soul and your spirit. Make friends with people who inspire you to become the best version of yourself everyday.

Three songs that speak to your soul?

Different songs speak to me at different moments but currently its;

- Sweeter by Leon Bridges
- Draw Me Close/Thy Will Be Done – Marvin Winans
- A Song For You – Donny Hathaway

What are you most proud of yourself for and why?

I'm so proud that I haven't quit on my dream to become a successful Recording Artist. There is so much of life that has happened that I could have stopped by now and just said I gave it my best shot and I don't think anyone would be mad at me but to still be on this journey, believing in something I've dreamt about as a little girl, I'm proud that I have chosen not to give up despite the hardships and obstacles, it shows me that I'm a pretty determined type of person, or maybe just a little bit crazy.

Sarah Orlarte

Who is Sarah? What are her origins and who would you best describe her as a woman of today?

A 42 years young Sydneysider who now calls Melbourne home and has done so since 2014. My origins are an equal mix of childhood trauma and a blessed life due to the love and devotion of my Grandparents who raised me following the death of my mother when I was a ten-year-old child. The woman I am today is shaped by my strength, resilience, gratitude, determination, compassion and willingness to "be-me" in the full knowledge that that may not be ok for some.

What is your profession? How did you end up in the industry you are in and what do you love about what you do?

I work in the field of Organisational Change Management and currently do this within the Financial services industry. Up until October of last year, I worked in this field though for a law enforcement agency in Victoria. My career really kicked off in the financial services industry going back to 1996. Though it was only in 2012 that I transitioned into the field of organisational change management. I was very fortunate to be working on a large-scale global transformation program at the time and worked closely with the change management team. Through that connection, I was mentored by an exceptional woman; Katrina Eadie. Katrina is the best there is when it comes to change management. Katrina took me under her wing between 2012 to 2014 teaching me and sharing with me everything she knew about the field. Katrina is a great example of women sponsoring and advocating for other women by bringing them up alongside her own successes and achievements. Some six years later I find myself loving the work more than ever and know I would not be the change practitioner I am today without the support and sponsorship of Katrina. What do I love about what I do? That is easy to answer – I love that I can support leaders and organisations to bring about positive change in the workplace with their people at the front-of-mind, every single time.

You are a woman of many talents and skills which is something that is so admired and inspirational to others. At the core of everything you do, you have an enormous love and spirit to live a life on your terms, fearless and unrelenting when it comes to doing things your way. Your love for your friends and family is undeniable as is your loyalty to being the best woman you can be at all times. You have overcome many hardships and challenges to get to where you are today and continue to survive and thrive. How do you balance the challenges of womanhood and your own personal evolution to make life work for you?

I have always invested heavily in therapy to help me with getting this balance right. I seriously could not get through a lot of stuff without my therapist – my therapist is my sounding board, my check in point and someone I trust implicitly when it comes to giving me some "hard truths" when I need to hear them. I am also prepared to get things wrong - I learn from it and take that lesson forward. Sometimes the harshest lessons are the ones that set us up for long-term success. And. I've come to terms with the fact that sometimes-making life work for you can result in losing people who can't accept the life you are creating for yourself. That took a while but that acceptance and being able to see it from their side has really opened my mind to the possibilities I can create for myself. It becomes limitless when you make life work for you on your terms and without the need to please others. When you can do that feel no resentment for those who don't sign up for it, your life truly becomes yours. Lastly, finding your voice and the commitment to making it heard in all aspects of life (career, friends, family and so on) has really served me well – only in the last few years have I really gotten to appreciate that, and I work on it every day

What do you think are the most important characteristics when it comes to creating a life on your terms and at times going against the usual stereotypes of life?

A willingness and commitment to living your truth, in the face of opposition and resistance to your truth. Continually checking in with yourself that you are living your truth and not slipping into doing things that you don't sit comfortably with. Backing yourself and your decisions when others will question you, judge you and seek to change your course because they are not comfortable. Never intentionally hurting someone else in the course of living your truth – through words, actions or lack of words and actions when they are needed. Having a high-degree of self-awareness, emotional intelligence and displaying empathy - especially for those opposing your truth. Being able to understand where they are coming from, I have found, takes away any bitterness or resentment for them not being supportive of the life you are living.

As a woman of creativity, passion, strength, ambition and determination, how would you best describe what success means to you and do you feel you have achieved success in your life?

I don't define my success through specific career achievements, material possessions, my bank balance or a carefully curated perception of me that I have created for others. Success to me means that when anyone who knows me is asked "is Sarah a good person, is she kind? Is she considerate? Is she honest"... they respond with "yes". I would also describe success for me as being able to back myself in the decisions I make and being willing to stand by those decisions under pressure and in the face of adversity.

What are the 5 things you cannot live without and why?

1. My girlfriends - My girlfriends fill my cup every day, they are my crutches when I can't stand up without support. When I reflect on the most challenging and difficult times I have experienced in my life, it is my girlfriends who have been the constant – they have been there to love me, nurture me and get me through to the other side where laughter, love and wonderful times become

possible again. My squad is small... but big in integrity, loyalty and a commitment to life-long and rich friendships. I can't imagine life without Kylie, Faten, Maxine, Therese, Mary, CJ and Crystal.

2. My niece Kirra-Lee - Kirra-Lee is the one person in this world who totally gets me in every single way. We connect on a deep spiritual level and have done so from day one. Despite the 27-year age difference, Kirra is my "go-to" for sharing news, experiences and my inner most thoughts that I don't share with even my closest girlfriends. It sounds like a lot to bear for a young woman, but she doesn't flinch, she is rock steady and teaches me so much about life, love and how to live "my best life" (to use one of her favourite clichés) . At 16 years of age, she possesses immense maturity and a deeply kind heart. Kirra's sense of self is inspiring, and she is someone I look to when I need to dig deep for my own sense of self. We have influenced each other in so many ways and I know that will continue as we both enter new phases of life. Importantly, no one can make me belly laugh like she can – her satirical humour talks to her

depth of maturity and awareness for herself and what is around her. At times I must remind myself she is indeed only 16 and not 36. Something I am sure her parents hold me accountable for. Like the time she proclaimed I love you "50,000 f**king dollars" – a take on Samantha Jones's quip in the first Sex and The City Movie!

3. My nephew Joshua - Joshua come into the world at just the right time for me. It was 1996 and I was uncertain about who I was, what my path would be, and truthfully, my decision making at the time was far from ideal. I've never felt a love so powerful as the first time I held Joshua in my arms. He was only a few weeks old, and I recall not letting him go for a whole day. If I wasn't holding him, I was changing his nappy or feeding him. Not long after, I moved in to live with Joshua, his mother, my Aunty and my grandmother. That young man was raised in a household of strong, determined and uniquely different women who loved him beyond measure. He gave my Grandmother an extra four years to her life, he sustained her and returned joy to her life. I will be forever grateful to Joshua for that gift of life.

Joshua also bonded the relationship his mother and I have. That bond would be tested frequently, she would wake to find Joshua not in his cot – only to find him snuggled in my bed with me. I would never say no to him (still can't) and would find every opportunity to "baby-sit". He has grown into an amazing young man – he is smart, warm, funny, kind, compassionate and someone who is just wonderful to share life with.

4. Music - Music provides me with endless opportunity to connect with my innermost feelings, to reflect on life, to share the joy of dancing with friends and having fun with friends with music as the backdrop. At times when I can't voice or articulate my own feelings, music steps in for me – it is equally therapeutic and a creator of joy. I turn to music when I am sad, I turn to music when I am happy, I turn to music when I need to focus and disconnect. Simply, it is the second heart beat that nurtures me. I am in constant awe that lyrics written by someone you will never know in your lifetime can so easily resonate with you, your experience and your emotions. Music makers are a life-line for me.

5. My dog Matilda Rose - It is true when they say, "a dog is a (wo)man's best friend". That unconditional love only a dog can give has got me through my darkest days in recent years. Matilda has been by my side at times when most humans would baulk at having to endure those days – it would be too much, not what they "signed up for". Matilda and her inner senses just leaned in more for me. Matilda is the best anxiety and depression treatment I could ever ask for, she is truly priceless. And, there is nothing better walking through the door to find Matilda over the moon to have her human "home".

The motto or mantra you live your life by?

It's a long one...Be kind. Be true to me. Be courageous. Be compassionate. Lean in and face the hardships. By doing these things, I will always be me.

What advice would you give to the teenage version of yourself, 18 years old and just about to embark on your life's journey?

You will continue to experience pain, loss and suffering. Though you are going to be ok through all of it. Never doubt your truth. Stay resolute in the moments it feels impossible to do so. You will establish amazing friendships and connections with so many remarkable people, all over the world. You will be blessed with an abundance of wonderful experiences – through travel, through your career and relationships. You will love and be loved. You will lose love, friendships and loved ones. You will also show yourself and others just how strong you are. The life you will have will be rich, you will not be short of experiences – both delightful and deeply sad experiences. You will discover that if you can be at peace with yourself, you will live a life of integrity, truth and will be so rewarded with amazing friends, deep love and a lifelong appreciation for yourself that will sustain you on those hard days.

Three songs that speak to your soul?

1. Talk to Her by India Arie
2. At Last by Etta James
3. Through the Fire by Chaka Khan

What are you most proud of yourself for and why?

I cannot reduce this response to a single thing. Equally, it is; the deep and unbreakable bonds I have with my niece and nephew. My friendships with my girlfriends. My commitments to living my truth. My ability to completely forgive others. My sense of self-awareness and empathy.

Deborah Price

Who is Deborah? What are her origins and who would you best describe her as a woman of today?

I was born in Sydney into a hard working close knit Australian family of four kids, three girls and a boy. Raised in Sydney's southern suburbs during the 70's, I have grown into a woman of immense strength and independence, who follows her own path, speaks her mind to a fault and has a strong sense of self and refutes judgement from others. When I speak her mind I believe that people who know my heart know that my intentions are true and that at the end of the day I only want the best for my loved ones.

What is your profession? How did you end up in the Entertainment Industry you are in and what do you love about what you do?

I am a business woman and an entreprenuer who run four successful home based businesses with the most successful being the children entertainment service. Within this service I host numerous children's events doing face painting, supplying party hire equipment and entertainers to numerous venues across Sydney and many private events. I started out at a local playcentre as a face painter and before long discovered my niche in the market for professional, artistic, well presented artists who used quality cosmetic grade face paint for children, which became the cornerstone of my business. Within 12 months of me starting my business I expanded my understanding and my knowledge of face painting and was able to grow from Debs Face Painting to Shire Face Painters, where I now have a group of successful face painters contracted to my business and also started a private facebook page dedicated to Sydney's best artists, that are willing to work together in a fun, positive and collaborative manner to help each other strive.

What I love most about my job is seeing the children's faces once I have completed a design, whether it be a glitter-filled butterfly or a scary skeleton for halloween, their faces light up and that is all the reward for me. A great moment of connection with children where their happiness and innocence is so refreshing.

You are a woman of many talents and skills which is something that is so admired and inspirational to others. Your passion, confidence, ambition and sense of purpose are truly inspiring and truly highlights the very essence of the woman you are. You are a woman who lives for and loves her family to the very core and has always maintained a positive and gratitude filled outlook on life that has managed to pull you through some very challenging times in your life. You are a fierce business owner whose entrepreneurial skills are second to none and a beloved member of your community that you support and empower through your incredible work ethic. You are also a proud wife and loving mother of two beautiful boys and foster mother to an amazing daughter that also shines a light on your

tireless effort to give love and support to children who need and deserve good and loving homes, which is something you have provided for many years. Your journey has been fraught with many adversities and challenges over the years and some difficult times that you have used to bolster yourself into a woman of light, compassion, strength and an admirable sense of purpose. How would you describe your journey as a wife, mother and successful entrepreneur and the balance to juggle it all?

I enjoy being a wife, mother and homemaker. I am very proud of the home I have worked so hard to build with my husband for our family and I strive to provide a safe, structured routined environment for my children and others that are brought into our lives through the foster system. I believe in taking one step at a time and not letting things way you down. Routine is key, and boundaries and routines for kids makes life less complicated. When new kids come into our home they just slip into our routine which just makes life easier. Everything is organised and colour coded to help streamline the cohesive structure of my home and I find children are able to thrive in this environment.

I cannot stress enough that weekly or regular date nights with your man are cheaper than counselling and so important to have that connection once a week with no interruptions. It's a moment to talk about what's going and of course reconnection and lots of relaxing time and love and light. If we miss a date night we certainly feel it and miss it.

What do you think are the most important characteristics when it comes to creating a life on your terms and at times going against the usual stereotypes of life?

I go against the usual stereotypes - not deliberately, it's just who I am. I listen to my gut and just like things to happen. I don't like the word no. Once I make a decision I stick to it and never falter. I go for what I want and make it happen. Going through Covid and isolation has helped me to slow down and focus on my family which has been a godsend. For most of my life I have always attempted to make the best of some pretty bad situations, allowing them to help me grow as a person. From my early years of being a molested child survivor, that in turn made me become a foster carer and someone that has a passion to want to help children. I have an ability to strive to turn the negatives into a positive and grow from the results. Learning to value and not validate myself through people, I found my way back through god and I acknowledge myself as a survivor and a woman of strength. I am a firm believer in a marriage where my husband looks after him for me and I look after me for him. I want my man to compliment me, not complicate me.

As a woman of passion, strength, loyalty and determination,, how would you best describe what success means to you and do you feel you have achieved success in your life?

Success to me is having a happy healthy family, close good loyal friends that have mine and my family's best interest at heart, good relationships, a good social network with women of substance in my world and people that I can go to in those moments where I might need extra support. I never sweat the small stuff and always fill my love tank spending time with those that I love and treat me right.

What are the 5 things you cannot live without and why?

1. God

2. My children

3. My family

4. Good friends

5. Meditation and me time.

The motto or mantra you live your life by?

Teamwork makes the dream work is our family mantra, in a general sense. In a marriage sense it would be " I'll look after me for you and you look after you for me" and " complement each other's lives don't complicate it".

What advice would you give to the teenage version of yourself, 18 years old and just about to embark on your life's journey?

- Count to ten before you make any decision.
- Put yourself first before others.
- You don't have to fix every man you meet.
- Do not change for anyone. Stay true to yourself.
- Do not compromise.
- Listen to your mother.

- Do not accept jealousy from others so choose your friends wisely.

- Slow down and stop rushing your life. There is plenty of time.

- Find yourself before entering any relationship.

- Breathe. Meditatre. Dont do Drugs.

- Basically don't do anything Deborah did when she was 18.

Three songs that speak to your soul?

1. Girls Just Wanna Have Fun - Cyndy Lauper
2. Give Me a Reason - Pink
3. How Great is our God - Chris Tomlins

What are you most proud of yourself for and why?

Being the strong woman I am but also learning to accept the moment when I'm not strong and sometimes allowing myself to be vulnerable to my husband(rarely) and my friends. As a 45 year old woman I am just learning to know that I can have vulnerable moments and that comes from a good marriage and establishing friendships with women I can trust. There is a strength in vulnerability and it helps my friends understand me more. I have an ability to connect and meet people where they are so I am proud of my solid perception of people too.

Jannike Seiuli

Who is Jannike? What are her origins and who would you best describe her as a woman of today?

First and foremost, I am a Mother and a wife. The greatest role I will ever be given in this life. Born in New Zealand to my Māori Mother and Samoan Father. I believe I am a strong, determined and creative woman.

What is your profession? How did you end up in the industry you are in and what do you love about what you do?

My profession is event management. Growing up in my teenage years, I was heavily involved with performing arts which led me to a new passion, events. With both my parents being community workers it gave me the opportunity to start work closely with events in my hometown. After many years of volunteering my time, I finally went and studied to receive the qualifications that I needed to support my experience in the field. What I love most about working in events is seeing the outcome of an event. Months/weeks of planning and then seeing it all come together. That's my favourite part.

You are a woman of many talents and skills which is something that is so admired and inspirational to others. As the founder and force behind the fashion forward Pacific Runway fashion shows as well as a host of various female first focussed events, you are a force to be reckoned with in more ways than one. Mother to three, soon to be four beautiful children sees you navigate the world between motherhood and entrepreneurship almost effortlessly, with your work ethic and love for family first something that is truly commendable. How do you balance the challenges of womanhood and your own personal evolution to make life work for you?

It is challenging at times to balance the two, but over the years I've had to learn to prioritise my time wisely.

My children have grown up in the events scene so they know when mummy is working and are often with me along the journey. My boys are older and love attending events and seeing what mummy has been working on. When my children are home after school hours, I don't do any business work so that they have my full attention. I will either do late nights or early mornings so that I'm not using the time that I should be present with my children. This is a balance that took me a while to perfect and still working on today.

What do you think are the most important characteristics when it comes to creating a life on your terms and at times going against the usual stereotypes of life?

To remain focused and really understanding your why? These 2 traits have helped me throughout the years. I have been questioned and challenged in the past as to what I was doing but that only fuelled the desire for me to work harder. Not everyone will understand your creativity and that's ok.

As a woman of creativity, passion, strength, ambition and determination, how would you best describe what success means to you and do you feel you have achieved success in your life?

Success to me is creating a platform that empowers all. I feel that I have been able to achieve this with Pacific Runway after 9 years. Everyone that takes part whether it's as a Designer, model, Makeup artist, Hair stylist, media etc, Pacific Runway is an event where our people feel proud to be a part of and representing their culture. As I watch the entire team and guests throughout the day/night it makes me extremely happy to see the smiles on peoples faces and the connections made between everyone that is involved. Each year is an experience that I will never forget.

What are the 5 things you cannot live without and why?

1. **Family** - I enjoy my life because of the people that are in it. They are my why in everything that I do.

2. **Camera** - I love capturing moments. At the end of each year we develop images to go into that year's Adventure book.

3. **Travel** - I love exploring the world and taking my children to see different parts of the world to experience different cultures and build more memories together.

4. **Music** - Music heals the soul. You can listen to songs of this era or from years ago and it automatically takes you to a place that you remember or creates a feeling.

5. **Journal** - Since a young age I have always loved keeping a journal to write down my thoughts and feelings each day.

The motto or mantra you live your life by?

"All our dreams can come true, if we have the courage to pursue them." - Walt Disney

What advice would you give to the teenage version of yourself, 18 years old and just about to embark on your life's journey?

Not to waste time. Study while you can and improve on your talents and skills.

Three songs that speak to your soul?

- I Smile - Kirk Franklin
- Closer - Goapele.
- I didn't know my own strength - Whitney Houston

What are you most proud of yourself for and why?

Building an Internationally recognised platform in Australia that can showcase the talents of our Creative people of the Pacific. Starting the Pacific Runway event in 2012 in our local community, I never imagined it to be where it is today.

Tamara Turrini

Who is Tamara? What are her origins and who would you best describe her as a woman of today?

Tamara is a mother, a wife, a teacher and a friend. I grew up in Berala with my father, brothers and grandparents and moved to Port Stephens for a period of time before returning to spend my high school years in Granville. I would describe myself as someone who is not easily pigeonholed, as I have many layers that have been constructed by varying experiences and influences in my life. Alongside my father, my grandparents helped raise my brothers and I. My grandparents taught me about modesty, commitment, loyalty and above all, the ability to be truly grateful. My father taught me that skills are worth more than materialistic objects and that strength comes from self reflection and growth.

What is your profession? How did you end up in the Education Community and what do you love about what you do?

I am a Primary School Teacher in Western Sydney. I became a teacher because I wanted to give ALL students, no matter what life experiences or background, an undeniable belief that they could do anything they set their minds to. I wanted to provide my students with ample opportunities that would help develop their confidence and capabilities. I struggled academically at school and performed really poorly in my HSC. Without my father's consistent encouragement to 'Hustle' my way to a better future, I would have believed that I was my poor score and not something much more than a number. I wanted students that struggled academically, to know that there are many types of intelligence and that your academic score does not define your worth or measure the characteristics needed to be successful in life. Basically, my philosophy as a teacher is 'No student left behind'. I love teaching because it's extremely fulfilling. I love teaching my students new skills and concepts and being able to encourage and support their developing personalities. I have learnt a lot about life in this profession and although it is mentally taxing, it also feels your soul with gratitude, hope and happiness.

You are a woman of many talents and skills which is something that is so admired and inspirational to others. As a teacher you are helping to shape and guide our children for the future and you are doing it with so much innovation, passion and care with your approach. As a wife and mother to two beautiful girls, you juggle the demands of being a hardworking teacher of primary aged students that you are truly passionate about as well at the ongoing demands of raising your girls into brave and fearless women just like their mother. Your outlook on life and teaching is one of positivity and change and even though your own personal journey has been one fraught with challenge you always strive to see the brighter side of life. How has the

balance between motherhood, teaching and your own personal evolution been for you?

Just like many mothers, I definitely feel the mental load of unrealistic expectations. Balancing work with family is always a challenge when you feel emotionally connected to both. I won the lottery twice when I gave birth to two healthy baby girls and I try my best to prioritize them first at every point. Teaching is about people, you are committed and what you do matters. You can't simply turn off your responsibilities as a teacher because your students need you too. I didn't want to get swept away in my teaching commitments (as you can easily do), so I decided to only work a few days a week. This has been wonderful for me and my family. I feel like I'm an active mother in my children's lives but I'm also giving them time to be independent in an environment designed to stimulate creativity and exploration. Due to this balance, I can continue my teaching career, where I can preserve a little of my own identity but still maintain and support my family unit. My personal evolution has definitely hit the hills in this marathon of life. I'm not seeing the glamorous iconic aspects of personal development during these early years of motherhood. I'm not displaying 'Martha

Stewart' capabilities in the household (which I thought I might), or becoming some type of fitness goddess. Instead, I'm developing patience. I'm learning to be grateful for all that I have. I'm recognising my ability to adapt and to ride out uncomfortable moments. I'm constantly reflecting on decisions, my own opinions and ideas. My personal evolution is happening deep within, affecting the core values and belief structures that I have. Becoming a mother brings great sacrifices (sleep, time, independence) but it brings rich lessons that force you to truly evolve.

What do you think are the most important characteristics when it comes to creating a life on your terms and at times going against the usual stereotypes of life?

- The ability to be grateful for what we have. Gratitude keeps you grounded and works on such a simplistic root level.

- The ability to truly reflect and question your own biases. Without reflection, we can't grow. I know that the more open minded I became the more I learnt about my own biases towards topics I knew nothing about. These biases perpetuate stereotypes.

- To have a strong sense of worth. Having a strong sense of worth creates an undential belief in yourself. When we feel worthy we are less likely to cut down those around us or feel as though we belong in any particular pigeonhole (destroying stereotypes).

- To listen to the voice in your heart over the doubt in your head. To create a life on your terms, I believe we need to ignore the doubt that creeps in over time and sits in the corner of our minds. Listen to that voice that is cheering you on and know that you are enough and that life is not a fixed destination.

- To create a life on your terms, I believe we should avoid comparing ourselves with others. When we compare our lives with others we risk paraphrasing someone else's artwork, rather than creating our own masterpiece. When mimicking other peoples' hopes and dreams then we are defined by someone elses definition of success.

As a woman of passion, strength, loyalty and determination, how would you best describe what success means to you and do you feel you have achieved success in your life?

I definitely feel as though I've achieved success in my life. Success looks different to everyone. I personally believe that being successful means that you have achieved some type of goal that you have set. Success can be large or small. It can be attached to many different aspects of your life. I have never been motivated by money nor do I really value materialistic things. Those that are/do, may find having a lot of money determines their success. When I speak about success, I usually refer to core values that I believe strongly in. I feel as though I am successful as I have healthy, loving and supportive relationships. I have a home to share with my family and I have a job that I love. These are all important to me, therefore I feel successful because I have achieved these things.

What are the 5 things you cannot live without and why?

1. My Family, they give me purpose, security and love

2. Coffee, I'm tired ALL the time!

3. My Car, I love the freedom that mobility gives me. I'm constantly taking the kids to new places, visiting family and friends and eating awesome food.

4. Music - It can soothe my soul or iit can energizes me

5. TV - It's my down time to relax, unwind and learn

The motto or mantra you live your life by?

"May your efforts be your own and your limits be unknown." - The Killers

What advice would you give to the teenage version of yourself, 18 years old and just about to embark on your life's journey?

I would tell 18 year old Tamara that she was right. The opinions of others should never change what you know to be real. I would tell her that life will always be a balance and that a growth mindset can change everything. I would tell her that she was beautiful and kind and that she had nothing to feel ashamed of. I would also tell her that sunscreen is key and that those long uni day naps will be something she dreams about in the years to come.

Three songs that speak to your soul?

- Be Still - The Killers
- Daughter - Pearl Jam
- Amazing Grace

What are you most proud of yourself for and why?

I am proud of the relationships I have built with my family, my friends and with myself. I feel as though I have learnt so much from everyone around me and that the older I get the more I can reflect and grow.

Lisa Viola

Who is Lisa? What are her origins and who would you best describe her as a woman of today?

My name means devoted one. I believe I was named aptly. I'm an Australian raised, biracial woman of African & Portugues descent.

What is your profession? How did you end up in the industry you work in and what do you love about what you do?

I'm a dancer, recording artist, actor and entrepreneur. I've been devoted to music and performance since I was a child, working professionally from the age of 14. I love what I do because:

- My work allows me to meet and collaborate with people from all walks of life
- My work challenges me to grow emotionally and spiritually
- My work has taught me courage

You are a woman of many talents and skills which is something that is so admired and inspirational to others. You are a respected singer / songwriter / dancer that has forged an incredible career that has seen you work with the global music industry on many levels and has helped shape you into the artist you have become. You are a proud woman of colour and culture who is always celebrating her African heritage through the very music you create. The road hasn't always been easy for you and you have overcome several challenges along the way, but through it all you are an independent warrior woman living life her way. How has the balance of your artistic self and your personal self been for you?

Right now my artistic self and personal self are pretty balanced. I no longer feel I have to be one or the other. I live my life in a way that I'm always nurturing both. It took me a while to get to that point.

What do you think are the most important characteristics when it comes to creating a life on your terms and at times going against the usual stereotypes of life?

I truly believe people already know deep down what is right for them. It's what people refer to as our inner voice. You need to actively do the soul searching to tap into that inner voice but once you hear it loud and clear you then need a whole lot of courage to act on it.

As a woman of passion, strength, loyalty and determination, how would you best describe what success means to you and do you feel you have achieved success in your life?

Success to me means growth. It's not finite. Personal, financial, educational, what ever it is if you're not growing then you're failing. I love setting goals and then kicking them. It's the journey between setting the goal and kicking it that growth happens. I'm in a state of success now and I hope to stay here until I die.

What are the 5 things you cannot live without and why?

1. Closest family and friends – What is life without love?

2. Meditation/Prayer – Realigns me spiritually/emotionally

3. Video calling – Whether it's for family or for work, it's where I spend a lot of time honoring and building relationships these days

4. My Macbook – It's basically my living, my creative and my entertainment

5. My iPhone – Same as above

The motto or mantra you live your life by?

BE KIND ALWAYS. Be humbled knowing that I am a part of something much greater than myself. No matter how great the issue, always remember that I'm not the only one who's gone through this.

What advice would you give to the teenage version of yourself, 18 years old and just about to embark on your life's journey?

You know what you were put here to do. Stop doubting yourself and go do it.

Three songs that speak to your soul?

I couldn't give you just three let alone 100 as it's a long list I'm constantly adding to, but currently I'd have to say these three. Body. Mind. Spirit.

1. Orion's Belt – Sabrina Claudio

2. Shoulda - Jamie Woon

3. Your Spirit – Tasha Cobbs

What are you most proud of yourself for and why?

I'm most proud of myself for my courage. Courage to go for the things I want, say the things I want to say and be who I am without needing external validation

www.ingramcontent.com/pod-product-compliance
Lightning Source LLC
Chambersburg PA
CBHW050306010526
44107CB00055B/2122